# God's Chosen People

*Knox Haddon, my baby boy, I am praying you join the multitude of stars of the sky that God promised to Abraham.*

# Contents

1. Introduction — *1*
2. Key Old Testament Passages — *8*
3. The Gospel According to Matthew — *29*
4. The Gospel According to Mark — *46*
5. The Gospel According to John — *67*
6. The Gospel According to Luke — *78*
7. Acts — *89*
8. Galatians — *101*
9. Romans — *112*
10. More Paul — *135*
11. The Letters — *152*
12. Synthesis and Conclusion — *159*
13. So What? — *164*

    Works Cited — *173*

Other Books by A. Blake White    *183*
About Cross to Crown Ministries    *184*

*1*

# Introduction

The relationship between Israel and the Church is nothing if not controversial. Entire systems of theology divide over it, and the passion is often white hot. Sharp and godly Christians come to very different conclusions. The temptation is to simply leave a controversial subject alone, but this topic is foundational to understanding our place in the story of God's grand redemptive purposes. It is not unimportant. Furthermore, I think this is a great "test case" for one's theology because it exposes whether or not we are truly committed to Scripture alone rather than to our theological presuppositions. The widespread disagreement I mentioned is due to letting theology inform exegesis rather than exegesis informing theology. I think the Scriptures are pretty clear about Israel and the Church. I hope to show that in this little book.

A. BLAKE WHITE

# DISPENSATIONALISM AND COVENANT THEOLOGY

First, a word about systems. If you are new to this discussion, it is helpful to know that there are various systems of theology that view this relationship in different ways. On the one hand, traditional Covenant Theology, with its over-arching covenant of grace, has tended to flatten out the old and new covenants and merely equate Israel and the Church. For them, the people of God are basically one and the same.[1]

This equation is overly simplistic. The Church did not begin until the coming of the Messiah and the pouring out of the Spirit at Pentecost. The body of Christ did not come into existence until Christ the head came.[2] It was a *new* entity.

As will be demonstrated, the New Testament Scriptures teach that the Church is a new covenant reality which fulfills old covenant Israel by virtue of union with Israel's Messiah. In the new covenant age, Gentiles are *included within* the Israel of God.[3]

On the other hand, traditional Dispensationalism totally separates Israel and the Church. One is the heavenly people

---

1. For more thorough overview, see Peter J. Gentry and Stephen J. Wellum, *Kingdom Through Covenant* (Wheaton: Crossway, 2012), 56-80. For example, Covenant theologian Keith Mathison writes, "The church existed in the Old Testament, but only in seed form as the true Israel" in *Dispensationalism: Rightly Dividing the People of God?* (Phillipsburg, NJ: P&R Publishing, 1995), 41.
2. John G. Reisinger, *Abraham's Four Seeds: A Biblical Examination of the Presuppositions of Covenant Theology and Dispensationalism* (Frederick, MD: New Covenant Media, 1998), 19.
3. The language is important here. We are not saying the Church replaces Israel. The label "replacement theology" is often thrown around as a way of dismissing the view out of hand. This is inclusion theology. A good analogy is a cocoon/butterfly relationship. Not a replacement, but a new phase of existence.

of God and the other is the earthly people of God. Never the twain shall meet.

Dispensationalism is hard to nail down nowadays, but according to Charles Ryrie's classic "textbook status" work, *Dispensationalism*, this distinction between Israel and the Church is the *sine qua non* of Dispensationalism.[4] For him and his followers, *this distinction* is what makes someone a Dispensationalist:

> This is probably the most basic theological test of whether or not a person is a dispensationalist, and it is undoubtedly the most practical and conclusive. The one who fails to distinguish Israel and the church consistently will inevitably not hold to dispensational distinctions; and one who does will.[5]

He goes on to write that, "The essence of Dispensationalism, then, is the distinction between Israel and the church."[6]

Beginning in the mid to late 1980s, a newer group emerged from within Dispensationalism that has come to be known as *Progressive Dispensationalism*. These theologians see more continuity between Israel and the Church, but they

---

4. For book length critical assessments, see Vern S. Poythress, *Understanding Dispensationalists* (Phillipsburg, NJ: P&R, 1994) and Mathison, *Dispensationalism*. To better understand the system, see Sam Storms, *Kingdom Come: The Amillennial Alternative* (Scotland: Mentor, 2013), 43-69; Gentry and Wellum, *Kingdom Through Covenant*, 40-56.
5. Charles C. Ryrie, *Dispensationalism* (Chicago: Moody, 2007), 46.
6. Ibid., 48.

still distinguish them in significant ways. According to them, the Church does inherit some of the blessings of the new covenant, like the gift of the Spirit and forgiveness of sins, but the promises of a restored nation and a land to dwell in await ethnic Israel in the millennium. These promises are not for the Church.[7]

Many wonder if *Progressive Dispensationalism* can still rightly be called *Dispensationalism*. Charles Ryrie, for one, is not a fan. It is interesting to note that the original 1966 version of his book was called *Dispensationalism Today,* but the revised 1995 version was changed to simply *Dispensationalism.* Implication: today, tomorrow, and forevermore. His gauntlet has been tossed. He considers the new developments as a "new departure" with "essential differences"[8] with his own "normative" Dispensationalism.[9] I'll leave it to them to work out who fits in the camp.

As will become apparent, our view of the relationship between the Church and Israel is closer to Covenant Theology than it is to Dispensationalism. I contend that the Dispensational view, contrary to Ryrie's claim that the distinction of Israel and the Church is "built on an inductive study of the use of two words, not a scheme superimposed on the Bible,"[10] is actually just that – an imposition of a

---

7. See Bruce Ware, "The New Covenant and the People(s) of God," in *Dispensationalism, Israel and the Church* ed. Craig A. Blaising and Darrell L. Bock (Grand Rapids: Zondervan, 1992), 68-97.
8. Ryrie, *Dispensationalism*, 80. See also 14, 18, 22, 36, 79-80, 101, 181, 189ff, 244.
9. Ibid., 210. He thinks that these developments "will most likely lead to covenantal premillennialism after the pattern of George E. Ladd."
10. Ryrie, *Dispensationalism*, 96.

theological system onto the text of Scripture. I hope to bear out this contention by examining several texts, and I hope you will imitate the Bereans and reexamine the Scripture to "see if these things are so" (Acts 17:10-11).

NEW COVENANT THEOLOGY

This book will come from the perspective of *New Covenant Theology*, which I have defined with the following seven points:[11]

1. There is one plan of God centered in Jesus Christ.
2. The Old Testament (OT) should be interpreted in light of the New Testament (NT).
3. The old covenant was temporary by divine design.
4. The old covenant law is a unit.
5. New covenant Christians are not under the law of Moses but under the "law" of Christ.
6. All members of the new covenant community are fully forgiven and indwelt by the Holy Spirit.
7. By virtue of union with Christ, the Church is the end-time Israel.

I don't claim to articulate *the* new covenant view of the relationship of Israel and the Church, but I do think the following approach is the most consistent with the hermeneutic of New Covenant Theology. Let me clearly lay out my cards before we dive in. Two major presuppositions

---

11. A. Blake White, *What Is New Covenant Theology? An Introduction* (Frederick, MD: New Covenant Media, 2012).

should be made explicit. First, and I do consider this *the* hermeneutical principle of New Covenant Theology, is that we unashamedly allow the NT to interpret the OT. Christians should learn OT theology from their Lord. We are disciples of Jesus in all of life, including hermeneutics. This book will let Jesus and His apostles teach us how to interpret the Hebrew Scriptures. Our hermeneutic of the OT is derived from theirs.[12]

Second, we unashamedly avow that Jesus Christ and His people are the fulfillment of all OT prophecy. Second Corinthians 1:20 cannot be improved on. "All the promises of God find their Yes in him." The Bible is about Jesus. It all points to Him. Moses wrote about Him (John 5:46). All the prophets spoke about Him (Luke 24:25). All the various streams of redemptive history flow to the feet of the royal Galilean.

As mentioned, I think this topic is worth pursuing because it is a great test case in how one lets the Bible inform one's theology, but I also think it is important because a large chunk of the NT is concerned with the unity of Jews and Gentiles in Christ. If our view of Jews and Gentiles separates them rather than unites them, I humbly submit that our view is at cross-purposes with the vision of the NT, and we

---

12. So France writes, "The New Testament writers consistently follow their Master's lead in looking to the Christian church for the fulfillment of the destiny of Israel. A *Christian* use of the prophecies of the Old Testament can hardly ignore the hermeneutical lead given by Jesus and his disciples." "Old Testament Prophecy and the Future of Israel: A Study of the Teaching of Jesus." *Tyndale Bulletin* (1975), 78.

need to re-examine our theological presuppositions in light of Scripture.

In some ways, I wrote this book to be an exegetical handbook. The plan is to simply walk through the Bible examining those key passages which answer the question of the relationship between the Church and Israel. It is a canonical approach. We'll be looking at passages from all over the canon of Scripture, but most of the effort will be on how the NT helps us interpret the OT and vice versa.[13] It will be an exercise in intertextual exegesis with reference to the people of God.

---

13. The Bible of the Apostles was the LXX. Where it may be helpful to see parallels, I have transliterated the Greek. Even if one does not know the language, one can see and hear the allusions through transliteration.

2

# Key Old Testament Passages

In this chapter, I will look at several significant OT texts which show how the Gentiles were always part of God's plan. Sometimes people assume that Gentile inclusion is only taught in the NT, but that's not the case.[1] There are strong and deep OT roots for seeing Gentiles being included in the people of God, that is, within Israel.[2]

---

1. Also, sometimes NCT is accused of downplaying the OT. I hope to show in this book that NCT relies strongly on the OT for our theological conclusion, just not isolated from the rest of the canon.
2. Christopher Wright comments, "The Old Testament has a vision of the people of God which will include, but not be confined to, ethnic Israelites: 'may nations will be joined with the Lord in that day and will become my people' (Zech. 2:11). This was not just an idea developed by the early church to legitimate the inclusion of Gentiles in response to Jewish rejection of Jesus. On the contrary, it was built into the 'genetic code' of Israel from the outset, as the New Testament's scriptural quotation and argumentation on this point show clearly. Just as the patriarchal family was only a stage in the development of the people of God, so national and territorial Israel in the Old Testament period was a stage toward the development of an international and global people of God. This is not just a 'Christian idea' but intrinsic to the Old Testament itself." "A Christian Approach to Old Testament Prophecy

## ABRAHAM

So much begins with Abraham.[3] He is promised that he would be the recipient of blessing, and in turn he and his family would be the mediators of blessing to the nations. Genesis 12:1-3 reads,

> Now the LORD said to Abram, 'Go from your country and your kindred and your father's house to the land that I will show you. And I will make of you a great nation, and I will bless you and make your name great, so that you will be a blessing. I will bless those who bless you, and him who dishonors you I will curse, and in you all the families of the earth shall be blessed'.

These promises are *foundational* to the rest of the storyline of Scripture.[4] Abraham is promised that he would become "the father of a multitude of nations" (Gen. 17:4). As we will see, this fatherhood exceeds the merely biological sense. If you are not Jewish, but claim Jesus as Lord, it is because God, in free and sovereign grace, called Abraham out of darkness into marvelous light and graciously gave him these wonderful promises.

Notice the *purpose* of the people of God. Right from their

---

Concerning Israel" in P.W.L. Walker, *Jerusalem Past and Present in the Purposes of God* (Cambridge: Tyndale House, 1992), 2-3.

3. I realize his name was changed later, but for the sake of consistency I am going with "Abraham" throughout.
4. John Stott writes, "It may truly be said without exaggeration that not only the rest of the Old Testament but the whole of the New Testament are an outworking of these promises of God." *Understanding the Bible* (Grand Rapids: Zondervan, 1984), 51.

formation, they were to be a "so that" people. They were blessed *so that* they would be a blessing. They would first be the recipients of blessing, then the mediators of blessing to the nations.[5] They are chosen for the sake of the world. God's one plan was always to rescue the world (bless the nations) through Abraham's offspring.[6] Their formation involved both privilege and obligation. He called them with the nations in mind.[7] Divine election is both about salvation and mission.[8]

Later in the narrative, God again says that all the nations of the earth will be blessed by the offspring of Abraham (Gen. 22:18). Note that "offspring" is singular here. God's purposes are to expand the family of Abraham beyond mere

---

5. Paul R. Williamson, *Sealed With an Oath: Covenant in God's Unfolding Purpose* (Downers Grove: InterVarsity Press, 2007), 82; C. Marvin Pate, J. Scott Duvall, J. Daniel Hays, E. Randolph Richards, W. Dennis Tucker Jr., and Preven Vang, *The Story of Israel: A Biblical Theology* (Downers Grove, IL: IVP Academic, 2004), 37-38.

6. Hans K. LaRondelle, *The Israel of God in Prophecy: Principles of Prophetic Interpretation* (Berrien Springs, MI: Andrews University Press, 1983), 91. Dispensationalists make the mistake of missing the purpose of Israel. Too often, they focus on Israel for Israel's sake. The purpose of Israel, from the beginning, was to bless the nations. Rob Dalrymple, *These Brothers of Mine: A Biblical Theology of Land and Family and a Response to Christian Zionism* (Eugene, OR: Wipf and Stock, 2105), 117-29. As Geerhardus Vos puts it, "The election of Abraham, and in the further development of things of Israel, was meant as a particularistic means toward a universalistic end." *Biblical Theology* (Grand Rapids: Eerdmans, 1963), 90. Michael Goheen, *A Light to the Nations: The Missional Church and the Biblical Story* (Grand Rapids: Baker Academic, 2011), 81; N.T. Wright pounds this home repeatedly in *Justification: God's Plan and Paul's Vision* (Downers Grove: IVP Academic, 2009),35, 65, 67, 94, 123, 129, 126, 132, 137, 196, 216; Wright, "A Christian Approach to Old Testament Prophecy," 1.

7. See my *Missional Ecclesiology* (Frederick, MD: New Covenant Media, 2013); Stephen G. Dempster writes, "Israel's calling is fundamentally missiological; its purpose for existence is the restoration of the world to its pre-Edenic state." *Dominion and Dynasty: A Theology of the Hebrew Bible* (Downers Grove: InterVarsity Press, 2003), 76; LaRondelle, *The Israel of God in Prophecy*, 91.

8. Goheen, *A Light to the Nations*, 29-32.

genealogy.⁹ We get a hint of this as the promise is reiterated to Jacob. In Genesis 27:29, Isaac blesses Jacob and tells him, "Let peoples serve you, and nations bow down to you. Be lord over your brothers, and may your mother's sons bow down to you. Cursed be everyone who curses you, and blessed be everyone who blesses you!" Peoples and nations will serve Jacob. His offspring will be like the dust of the earth and will spread out toward the west, the east, the north, and the south (Gen. 28:14). Jacob's offspring will not merely be limited to genealogical offspring. God has grander purposes—the nations will be included.

Keep in mind that the storyline of Scripture doesn't begin with Abraham but with Adam. God cursed the serpent and said that a singular offspring of the woman would crush the serpent's head. Then Abraham is given these promises and is told that kings would come from him (Gen. 17:6, 16). Jacob is promised "a nation and a company of nations shall come from you" (Gen. 35:11-12).¹⁰ Only with the greatest difficulty can "a nation and a company of nations" be restricted to merely physical offspring. The plot of Genesis is preparing us to expect a singular descendant of the woman (and of Abraham) who will bring blessing to the nations. Through the gracious rule of this singular offspring, the nations will be part of

---

9. See Paul Williamson's superb article, "Abraham, Israel, and the Church," *The Evangelical Quarterly* 72.2, 99-118.
10. See the helpful articles by Chee-Chiew Lee, "[Nations] and the Abrahamic Promise of Blessings for the Nations," *JETS* 52, no. 3 (Sept 2009): 467-82 and Daniel S. Diffey, "The Royal Promise in Genesis," *Tyndale Bulletin* 62.2 (2011): 313-16.

Abraham's offspring. Jacob's family will not only be the nation of Israel, but an assembly of nations.

At the end of his life, Jacob blesses his sons and tells Judah that the scepter will not depart from him and "the obedience of the peoples belongs to Him" (Gen. 49:10). The book of beginnings sets up the thesis of this study nicely. God will deal with evil and include all the nations of the earth in the family of Abraham by blessing them as they submit to the rule of the singular royal offspring of the woman/Abraham/Jacob/Judah.[11] Beautiful!

## EXODUS

Much could be said of Exodus, but for our purposes we will limit ourselves to one passage. Before the giving of the Law, God says,

> You yourselves have seen what I did to the Egyptians, and how I bore you on eagles' wings and brought you to myself. Now therefore, if you will indeed obey my voice and keep my covenant, you shall be my treasured possession among all peoples, for all the earth is mine; and you shall be to me a kingdom of priests and a holy nation. These are the words that you shall speak to the people of Israel. (Exod. 19:4–6)

God rescued His people with the purpose of them

---

11. For more on "seed" in Genesis, see T.D. Alexander, "Genealogies, Seed and the Compositional Unity of Genesis," *Tyndale Bulletin* 44.2, 255-367; idem, "Royal Expectation in Genesis to Kings," *Tyndale Bulletin* 49.2, 191-212.

becoming a "kingdom of priests." What do priests do? They mediate between God and the people. They were to be holy, distinct, so as to draw the attention of the nations to their God. As in Genesis 12, the missional vocation of Israel is reaffirmed.[12] They exist for the nations. "Israel's election was not a rejection of other nations but was explicitly for the sake of all nations."[13]

## THE PROPHETS

[14]Isaiah is "the high point of Old Testament prophecy."[15] He is also a prophet very concerned with the nations because,

---

12. Williamson writes, "The whole nation has thus inherited the responsibility formerly conferred on Abraham – that of mediating God's blessing to the nations of the earth... Thus understood, the goal of the Sinaitic covenant was the establishment of a special nation through which Yahweh could make himself known to all the families of the earth" *Sealed With an Oath*, 97; Andreas J. Kostenberger and Peter T. O'Brien, *Salvation to the Ends of the Earth: A Biblical Theology of Mission* (Downers Grove: InterVarsity Press, 2001), 34-36; Dempster, *Dominion and Dynasty*, 101-04; Gentry and Wellum, *Kingdom Through Covenant*, 303-04.
13. Christopher J.H. Wright, *The Mission of God: Unlocking the Bible's Grand Narrative* (Downers Grove: IVP Academic, 2006), 65. Later, he writes, "As the people of YHWH they would have the historical task of bringing the knowledge of God to the nations, and bringing the nations to the means of atonement with God. The Abrahamic task of being a means of blessing to the nations also put them in the role of priests in the midst of the nations." *The Mission of God*, 331 371-72.
14. For further and deeper study of some of these passages, see *Wright Mission of God* 489-500; LaRondelle, *The Israel of God in Prophecy*, 81-96; Williamson, *Sealed With an Oath*, 146-81: Kostenberger and O'Brien, *Salvation to the Ends of the Earth*, 25-54: Jeremy R. Treat, *The Crucified King: Atonement and Kingdom in Biblical and Systematic Theology* (Grand Rapids: Zondervan, 2014), 68-86; Gentry and Wellum, *Kingdom Through Covenant*, 433-530; William J. Dumbrell, *The Faith of Israel: A Theological Survey of the Old Testament* (Grand Rapids: Baker Academic, 2002), 115-32; idem., *Covenant and Creation: A Theology of the Old Testament Covenants* (Carlisle, PA: Paternoster Press, 1984), 190-200; Wright, *The Mission of God*, 235-43, 484-500, 520; G.K. Beale, *A New Testament Biblical Theology: The Unfolding of the Old Testament in the New* (Grand Rapids: Baker Academic, 2011), 656-69; Pate, et al., *The Story of Israel*, 88-103.
15. Treat, *The Crucified King*, 37.

of course, *God* is very concerned with the nations. We will highlight five important passages from this great prophet, pulling in help from other prophets where profitable.

First, Isaiah 2:2-3, which reads,

> It shall come to pass in the latter days that the mountain of the house of the LORD shall be established as the highest of the mountains, and shall be lifted up above the hills; and all the nations shall flow to it, and many peoples shall come, and say: 'Come, let us go up to the mountain of the LORD, to the house of the God of Jacob, that he may teach us his ways and that we may walk in his paths.' For out of Zion shall go the law, and the word of the LORD from Jerusalem.

This prophecy is often viewed as being fulfilled only way off in our future at the second coming of Christ. As with so much of prophecy, there is an "already/not yet" aspect, but we know that this prophecy has been inaugurated with the first coming of Christ because Peter quotes from it in Acts 2:17[16] to introduce *Joel's* prophecy of the coming of the

---

16. Graeme Goldsworthy writes, "I want to assert categorically that ALL prophecy was fulfilled in the gospel event at the first coming of Jesus. There was only one coming projected in prophecy, yet somehow we must understand the New Testament perspective of two coming as consonant with this. There is a tendency to try to differentiate Old Testament prophecies of the end into two groups, those applying to the first coming and those applying to the second coming… Nothing will happen at the return of Christ that has not already happened in him at his first coming. All the expectations of the Old Testament have come to fulfillment IN HIM. And this has happened FOR US." *Preaching the Whole Bible as Christian Scripture* (Grand Rapids: Eerdmans, 2000), 93.

Spirit and the rescue of Israel. Peter begins with "in the last days" (*en tais eschatais hemerais*), which is not found in Joel but in Isaiah 2. In fact, this exact phrase is only found in these two places in the Greek OT and NT: Isaiah 2 and Acts 2. So Peter is showing us that this promise of nations flowing into Zion in Isaiah 2 and the rescue of Israel in Joel 2 are being fulfilled at Pentecost as the glory cloud falls upon the new covenant Church.[17] All nations are now streaming to the New Jerusalem. In NT typology, both Jesus (John 2:19-21) and the body of Jesus (1 Cor. 3:16, 6:19, 2 Cor. 6:16-7:1) are the new and true temple, and the nations are flowing into it as the gospel is proclaimed and obeyed.

The second important passage is Isaiah 19:18-25, which reads,

> In that day there will be five cities in the land of Egypt that speak the language of Canaan and swear allegiance to the LORD of hosts. One of these will be called the City of Destruction. In that day there will be an altar to the LORD in the midst of the land of Egypt, and a pillar to the LORD at its border. It will be a sign and a witness to the LORD of hosts in the land of Egypt. When they cry to the LORD because of oppressors, he will send them a savior and defender, and deliver them. And the LORD will make himself known to the Egyptians, and the Egyptians will know the LORD in

---

17. Alan J. Thompson, *The Acts of the Risen Lord Jesus: Luke's Account of God's Unfolding Plan*. NSBT (Downers Grove, IL: InterVarsity Press, 2011), 128.

that day and worship with sacrifice and offering, and they will make vows to the LORD and perform them. And the LORD will strike Egypt, striking and healing, and they will return to the LORD, and he will listen to their pleas for mercy and heal them. In that day there will be a highway from Egypt to Assyria, and Assyria will come into Egypt, and Egypt into Assyria, and the Egyptians will worship with the Assyrians. In that day Israel will be the third with Egypt and Assyria, a blessing in the midst of the earth, whom the LORD of hosts has blessed, saying, 'Blessed be Egypt my people, and Assyria the work of my hands, and Israel my inheritance'.

This no doubt would have been a puzzling passage to many a Pharisee. I can envision a Pharisaic father moving straight from Isaiah 18 to Isaiah 20 during Hebrew homeschool in order to avoid unanswerable questions from a curious child. After all, Egypt and Assyria were the quintessential enemies of Israel. Yet, in the future there would be an "altar" to the Lord in Egypt. When the poor Egyptians cry out, Yahweh will send them a savior. Gentile nations will be included in the people of God. The Lord says that Egypt will be called "My people" and Assyria will be called "My handiwork." OT scholar Chris Wright observes, "The shock of reading 'Egypt' immediately after 'my people' (instead of the expected Israel) and of putting Israel third on the list is palpable. Yet there it is. The arch enemies of Israel will be absorbed into the identity, titles and privileges of

Israel and share in the Abrahamic blessing of the living God, YHWH."[18]

The third important passage is Isaiah 49:1-7 (cf. Isa. 42:1-6):

> Listen to me, O coastlands, and give attention, you peoples from afar. The LORD called me from the womb, from the body of my mother he named my name. He made my mouth like a sharp sword; in the shadow of his hand he hid me; he made me a polished arrow; in his quiver he hid me away. And he said to me, 'You are my servant, Israel, in whom I will be glorified.' But I said, 'I have labored in vain; I have spent my strength for nothing and vanity; yet surely my right is with the LORD, and my recompense with my God.' And now the LORD says, he who formed me from the womb to be his servant, to bring Jacob back to him; and that Israel might be gathered to him – for I am honored in the eyes of the LORD, and my God has become my strength – he says: 'It is too light a thing that you should be my servant to raise up the tribes of Jacob and to bring back the preserved of Israel; I will make you as a light for the nations, that my salvation may reach to the end of the earth.' Thus says the LORD, the Redeemer of Israel and his Holy One, to one deeply despised, abhorred by the nation, the servant of rulers:

---

18. Wright, *Mission of God*, 493. Robertson notes, "It is almost as though the land of Israel is to be bypassed!" *The Israel of God*, 21.

'Kings shall see and arise; princes, and they shall prostrate themselves; because of the LORD, who is faithful, the Holy One of Israel, who has chosen you'.

We will bump into Isaiah 40-66 many times in this book. It is hugely important to the NT writers. Some of the Patristics saw this and called it the "Fifth Gospel." In Isaiah 40 and following, we see God's grand promises of a "new exodus."[19] God would return, defeat Israel's enemies, make a way, and lead His redeemed people to freedom where God would reign as King and dwell with His people again. These promises were yet unfulfilled in the first century, even though many Jews had returned to the land.

Isaiah 49 is about the Servant of the Lord bringing salvation to Israel. In this larger section of Isaiah, there is a tension about the Servant. In places, the Servant is the nation (Isa. 41:8, 42:18-19), but the Servant is also an individual working on behalf of the nation. Isaiah 49 speaks of the Servant—Israel—who sums up and restores Israel.[20] This Servant will "bring Jacob back" to Yahweh so that "Israel might be gathered to him" (Isa. 49:5). This individual Servant will raise up the tribes of Jacob, restore Israel, and be a light to the nations, to be the salvation of the Lord to the ends of the

---

19. LaRondelle writes, "More than any other prophet's words, Isaiah's predictive prophecies of chapters 40-66 stand out as the great promises of Israel's restoration after the Assyrian-Babylonian exile." *The Israel of God in Prophecy*, 87.
20. Ibid., 93. Thompson writes, "The Servant in Isaiah 49 both represents Israel ('you are my servant, Israel', 49:3), embodying all that Israel should have been, and yet is also distinct from Israel since the task of the Servant is to restore Israel (49:5-6)." *The Acts of the Risen Lord Jesus*, 118.

earth (Isa. 49:6). It would be too "light a thing" if the Servant only restored Jacob (Isa. 49:6), so He will include the nations in His kingdom restoration project. He will make them an effective light to the nations. When Jacob is brought back, He will include the ends of the earth.

As we have begun to see and will see numerous times, the NT helps us determine the fulfillment of OT prophecy. The book of Acts makes use of this passage a number of times, which shouldn't surprise us. Though we will look at it in more detail below, for now notice how Jesus alludes to Isaiah 49 in the first chapter of Acts.

Acts 1:8 reads, "But you will receive power when the Holy Spirit has come upon you, and you will be my witnesses in Jerusalem and in all Judea and Samaria, and to the end of the earth." The last phrase "end of the earth" (*heōs eschatou tēs gēs*) comes straight from Isaiah 49:6, which reads, "I will make you as a light for the nations, that my salvation may reach to the end of the earth" (*heōs eschatou tēs gēs*). The ministry and mission of the early Church is fulfilling the Servant's vocation. As Jews *and Gentiles* are brought to faith in Christ, the Kingdom is being restored to Israel, just like Isaiah 49 says. This fits right with how Luke describes what Acts is all about: "In the first book, O Theophilus, I have dealt with all that Jesus began to do and teach." Luke is about what Jesus *began* to do. Acts will be about what He is continuing to do. The book of Acts is about what Jesus the Servant—through His body—is doing. So rather than "The Acts of the Apostles," perhaps "The Acts of the Risen Lord Jesus" is a better title.[21]

Next, notice how Paul and Barnabas apply Isaiah 49:6 in Acts 13:46-49:

> And Paul and Barnabas spoke out boldly, saying, 'It was necessary that the word of God be spoken first to you. Since you thrust it aside and judge yourselves unworthy of eternal life, behold, we are turning to the Gentiles. For so the Lord has commanded us, saying, 'I have made you a light for the Gentiles, that you may bring salvation to the ends of the earth'. And when the Gentiles heard this, they began rejoicing and glorifying the word of the Lord, and as many as were appointed to eternal life believed. And the word of the Lord was spreading throughout the whole region.

Here again, the ministry of the Servant who restores Israel-plus-the-nations is applied to the ministry of the Apostles. *They* are a light to the nations. Again, Jesus is a corporate person.[22] We are *in Him*. The body is organically related to the head.

One more passage is worth mentioning before we move on to the next Isaiah passage. In Luke's first volume, he records Zechariah's prophecy, which is full of OT prophecy (Luke 1:67-79). Zechariah blesses God for visiting and redeeming His people, for raising up a horn of salvation in the house of David, and for keeping His promises to the

---

21. So Thompson, *The Acts of the Risen Lord Jesus*.
22. LaRondelle, *The Israel of God in Prophecy*, 93-94.

Fathers, the oath He swore to Abraham. This child will go and give knowledge of salvation to His people and will "give light to those who sit in darkness and in the shadow of death, to guide our feet into the way of peace" (Luke 1:79). One only had to read a few more chapters to see that the ministry of this King will include Gentiles. "His people" are the ones who to respond rightly to Him. Jesus is almost killed right off the bat for claiming that Isaiah 61 was fulfilled in Him and for pointing out God's grace to non-Israelites: Zarephath of Sidon and Naaman the Syrian (Luke 4:16-30).

The fourth passage from Isaiah is Isaiah 56:1-7:

> Thus says the LORD: 'Keep justice, and do righteousness, for soon my salvation will come, and my righteousness be revealed. Blessed is the man who does this, and the son of man who holds it fast, who keeps the Sabbath, not profaning it, and keeps his hand from doing any evil.' Let not the foreigner who has joined himself to the LORD say, 'The LORD will surely separate me from his people'; and let not the eunuch say, 'Behold, I am a dry tree.' For thus says the LORD: 'To the eunuchs who keep my Sabbaths, who choose the things that please me and hold fast my covenant, I will give in my house and within my walls a monument and a name better than sons and daughters; I will give them an everlasting name that shall not be cut off. 'And the foreigners who join themselves to the LORD, to minister to him, to love the name of the LORD, and to be his servants,

everyone who keeps the Sabbath and does not profane it, and holds fast my covenant – these I will bring to my holy mountain, and make them joyful in my house of prayer; their burnt offerings and their sacrifices will be accepted on my altar; for my house shall be called a house of prayer for all peoples'.

Here we have a prophecy of a future restored Jerusalem when God brings salvation.[23] The ESV subtitle for this section is "Salvation for Foreigners." Yes and amen. Here, the Lord encourages the foreigners. They ought not worry about being separated from the people of God if they have joined themselves to the Lord (Isa. 56:3). To the faithful foreign eunuchs, the Lord will give a name in His house even better than sons and daughters. We see this begin to be fulfilled in Acts 8 when the biblically curious Ethiopian eunuch providentially turns to Isaiah 53 and is baptized by Philip. This, of course, overturns the old covenant stipulation that eunuchs be excluded from the assembly of the Lord (Deut. 23:1-7). The new covenant will bring a new day and this is good news for eunuchs and the nations.

Isaiah goes on to say that foreigners will join themselves to the Lord to minister to Him. The word for "minister" is most often used of priests. Foreigners *will become priests?* Incredible! We will treat this more in the fifth and final passage from Isaiah below.

Zechariah says the same thing: "Sing and rejoice, O

---

23. Ibid., 87-88.

daughter of Zion, for behold, I come and I will dwell in your midst, declares the LORD. And many nations shall join themselves to the LORD in that day, and shall be my people. And I will dwell in your midst, and you shall know that the LORD of hosts has sent me to you" (Zech. 2:10-11). Non-Israelite nations will be joined to the Lord. They will be His people. "This is not 'Israel plus the nations' but 'the nations as Israel,' one people belonging to God."[24] This idea of people being joined to the Lord points forward to union with the Messiah. Though we don't want to get ahead of ourselves here, one cannot help but think of Galatians 3:29: "And if you are Christ's, then you are Abraham's offspring, heirs according to promise."

More on Galatians later, but this also reminds the attentive reader of Psalm 87 and Ezekiel 47. In the former, we learn that Yahweh "loves the gates of Zion more than all the dwelling places of Jacob" (Psa. 87:2). Glorious things of Zion are spoken. Psalm 87:4-7 reads,

> Among those who know me I mention Rahab and Babylon; behold, Philistia and Tyre, with Cush – 'This one was born there,' they say. And of Zion it shall be said, 'This one and that one were born in her'; for the Most High himself will establish her. The LORD records as he registers the peoples, 'This one was born there.' Singers and dancers alike say, 'All my springs are in you'.

---

24. Wright, *The Mission of God*, 498.

Rahab is a nickname for Egypt, so here like in Isaiah 19, we have two of Israel's archenemies—Egypt and Babylon—among others, who will be born in Zion, the blessed city of God. This is what Paul means when he speaks of Jerusalem our mother (Gal. 4:26). Isaiah says that God registers these foreigners as having been born in the Jerusalem above. These Gentiles were obviously not naturally born in Zion, but the Lord elects them to Zionic citizenship.[25] They were born "not of blood nor of the will of the flesh nor of the will of man, but of God" (John 1:13). In the new covenant age, Gentiles will be included with the one people of God.

Ezekiel 47:21-23 reads,

> So you shall divide this land among you according to the tribes of Israel. You shall allot it as an inheritance for yourselves and for the sojourners who reside among you and have had children among you. They shall be to you as native-born children of Israel. With you they shall be allotted an inheritance among the tribes of Israel. In whatever tribe the sojourner resides, there you shall assign him his inheritance, declares the Lord GOD.

Here God tells Israel that the Gentiles (sojourners) will be as native-born children of Israel. Non-Jews will be allotted an inheritance. At one point in their former history, Israel herself

---

25. Gentry and Wellum write, "Zion becomes the mother of the nations, not through natural birth but through Yahweh's own determination and election." *Kingdom Through Covenant*, 452.

was considered a sojourner. Leviticus 25:23 says, "For you are strangers and sojourners with me." So we see from these verses that in the coming age, non-Israelites will be included in the Israel of God.

The fifth and final passage from Isaiah comes from Isaiah 66:18-21:

> For I know their works and their thoughts, and the time is coming to gather all nations and tongues. And they shall come and shall see my glory, and I will set a sign among them. And from them I will send survivors to the nations, to Tarshish, Pul, and Lud, who draw the bow, to Tubal and Javan, to the coastlands far away, that have not heard my fame or seen my glory. And they shall declare my glory among the nations. And they shall bring all your brothers from all the nations as an offering to the LORD, on horses and in chariots and in litters and on mules and on dromedaries, to my holy mountain Jerusalem, says the LORD, just as the Israelites bring their grain offering in a clean vessel to the house of the LORD. And some of them also I will take for priests and for Levites, says the LORD.

This is a fascinating conclusion to Isaiah's vision of the new exodus. All nations and tongues will come and see the glory of the Lord. God will set a sign among them (likely the cross[26]). Survivors will be sent among the nations and will

---

26. Ibid., 458.

bring people from all nations "as an offering to the Lord" (Isa. 56:20). The Gentiles will be brought in as an offering. Sound familiar? Paul draws on this passage in the book of Romans. In Romans 15:16, Paul says that grace was given to him "to be a minister of Christ Jesus to the Gentiles in the priestly service of the gospel of God, so that the offering of the Gentiles may be acceptable, sanctified by the Holy Spirit." Paul, the pastor-missionary, views his work in light of Isaiah's vision. His hopes are to preach the gospel far and wide and present Gentile Christians as an offering to the one true God.

I think this conclusion to Isaiah's second exodus vision informs other NT passages as well. The Gentiles will be brought into Israel as a pleasing offering. In Romans 12:1, in light of the gospel glories of the first 11 chapters, the Romans (Gentiles) are exhorted to "present their bodies as a living sacrifice, holy and acceptable to God, which is your spiritual worship." This verse is full of cultic language. In the old covenant, worship was localized and only performed by particular people. That's why Jesus told the Samaritan woman at the well that an hour was coming when people would neither worship in Jerusalem nor in Samaria, but in Spirit and truth. Here in Romans 12, Paul universalizes worship. Worship is no longer merely done at the temple. And all do it. All the time. Paul secularizes the sanctuary and sanctifies the secular. Now, all of life is worship. Before, priests "presented" dead sacrifices. Now, everyone presents their bodies, that is, their whole selves to God. *Living* sacrifices. We give up our lives and now live for Him. It is no longer what a person gives, but the giver Himself. The inclusion of Gentiles is seen as an offering to the Lord.

This vision in Isaiah 66 of survivors being sent to gather in "all nations and tongues" also informs John 11. There, John records Caiaphas the high priest prophesying that "Jesus would die for the nation, and not for the nation only, but also to gather into one the children of God who are scattered abroad" (John 11:51-52). The death of Jesus is what accomplished the new exodus that Isaiah spoke about (Luke 9:31). And Caiaphas speaks of that death being for Israel, but not just Israel, but all the children of God scattered. Some say that this merely refers to ethnic Jews scattered abroad, but John has already made it clear that the children of God include more than just Jews, but any who trust in Jesus: "But to all who did receive him, who believed in his name, he gave the right to become children of God, who were born, not of blood nor of the will of the flesh nor of the will of man, but of God" (John 1:12-13).

At the end of Isaiah 66, strikingly, the Lord says that He will take some of these Gentiles "for priests and for Levites" (Isa. 66:21). Non-Levites will be taken for Levites! Of course, we already saw this. Isaiah 56:6 spoke of foreigners joining themselves to the Lord and "ministering" to Him, which is an old covenant word for priestly service. Gentiles will become priests. One should not be surprised to see this truth taught all over the NT. We'll look at 1 Peter in more detail below as well, but for now notice the allusion to this vision: "you yourselves like living stones are being built up as a spiritual house, to be a holy priesthood, to offer spiritual sacrifices acceptable to God through Jesus Christ" (1 Pet. 2:5). Christians are the new temple, the new dwelling place of God (Eph. 4:21-22), living stones being built into a spiritual house to be a holy priesthood that offers acceptable sacrifices. In a typologically-glorious mixing of old covenant metaphors, new covenant Christians are the temple and the priests who worship in the temple.

Again, as Isaiah 56:7 put it, the foreigners please the Lord with their offerings and sacrifices. Philippians 4:18 describes the financial support of the Gentile Philippians as "a fragrant offering, a sacrifice acceptable and pleasing to God." Hebrews 13:15-16 speaks of our praise and our sharing of resources as "sacrifices" that are pleasing to God. As I hope is clear, Isaiah's vision of the sacrifice of Gentiles began to come to fulfillment in the first coming of Jesus and the growth of the Church.[27]

---

27. Although Israel did return to the land, these grand promises had not yet been fulfilled, which is clear from the minor prophets, Jewish history, and the teaching of the NT. See P.W.L. Walker, *Jesus and the Holy City: New Testament Perspectives on Jerusalem* (Grand Rapids: Eerdmans, 1996), 44, 283-84.

*3*

# The Gospel According to Matthew

New Testament scholar Richard Hays says that each of the Gospels "narrates the story of Jesus as the continuation and fulfillment of Israel's story."[1] The Gospels present Jesus as the solution to the sordid story of Israel and the fulfillment of Israel's hopes.[2] Matthew is probably the clearest of all, which makes sense given his primarily Jewish audience. He quotes the OT more than 60 times!

Matthew is very intentional in the way he starts his Gospel.

---

1. Richard B. Hays, "The Canonical Matrix of the Gospels," in *The Cambridge Companion to the Gospels*, ed. Stephen C. Barton (Cambridge University Press, 2006), 53. R.T. France agrees: "In the coming of Jesus of Nazareth all God's purposes for his people, declared and illustrated throughout the writings of the OT and the history of Israel, are coming to their destined fulfillment." *The Gospel of Matthew* (Grand Rapids: Eerdmans, 2007), 25.
2. France writes, "I have found no instance where Jesus expects a fulfillment of Old Testament prophecy other than through his own ministry, and certainly no suggestion of a future restoration of the Jewish nation independent of himself. He himself is the fulfillment to which Old Testament prophecy points, the ultimate horizon of the prophetic vision." "Old Testament Prophecy and the Future of Israel," 58; Pate et al., *The Story of Israel*, 280.

He shows that Jesus sums up Israel in himself. He gives us a Genesis (Matt. 1:1), an Exodus (Matt. 2:15), a passing through the Jordan (Matt. 3:13-17), a temptation in the wilderness (Matt. 4:1-11). Then like Moses in Deuteronomy, Jesus goes "up on a mountain" (Matt. 5:1) to "lay down the law" (Matt. 5:17-48) before commencing on a kingly and prophetic ministry that ends with an exile (cross) and subsequent restoration (resurrection).[3] The story of Israel is being replayed in the story of Israel's Messiah. His life takes the shape of Israel's story.[4] As we saw above in Isaiah 49, He is the true Israel who will restore Israel.

## A JEWISH (AND GENTILE) GENEALOGY?

Matthew strategically opens his story with the words: "The book of the genealogy of Jesus Christ, the son of David, the son of Abraham" (Matt. 1:1). The word "genealogy" in Greek is *geneseōs*, which means "genesis." The book of the Genesis of Jesus Christ. The Messiah is bringing about a new Genesis, a whole new world.

What a way to begin the story of Jesus! He wants his readers to know right from the start what his agenda is, namely to show that Jesus is the fulfillment of the hopes of

---

3. S. Motyer, "Israel (nation)" in *New Dictionary of Biblical Theology* ed. T. Desmond Alexander, Brian S. Rosner (Downers Grove: InterVarsity Press, 2000), 585; N.T. Wright, *The New Testament and the People of God* (Minneapolis: Fortress Press, 1992), 402; Walker, *Jesus and the Holy City*, 45.
4. R.T. France, *Jesus the Radical: A Portrait of the Man They Crucified* (Vancouver: Regent College Publishing, 1989), 53, 144-45; J.R. Daniel Kirk, "Conceptualising Fulfilment in Matthew," *Tyndale Bulletin* 59.1, 90-94: Thomas R. Schreiner, *New Testament Theology: Magnifying God in Christ* (Grand Rapids: Baker Academic, 2008), 70-79

Israel. The bridge from the story of Israel to the story of Jesus is a family tree. By beginning this way, Matthew is saying, "If you wish to understand Jesus, you must see Him as the completion of this story."[5]

Jesus is the son of David. Those three little words "son of David" bring to mind a host of OT promises. The most notable, of course, are the promises given to David in 2 Samuel 2:7:9-17:

> And I have been with you wherever you went and have cut off all your enemies from before you. And I will make for you a great name, like the name of the great ones of the earth. And I will appoint a place for my people Israel and will plant them, so that they may dwell in their own place and be disturbed no more. And violent men shall afflict them no more, as formerly, from the time that I appointed judges over my people Israel. And I will give you rest from all your enemies. Moreover, the LORD declares to you that the LORD will make you a house. When your days are fulfilled and you lie down with your fathers, I will raise up your offspring after you, who shall come from your body, and I will establish his kingdom. He shall build a house for my name, and I will establish the throne of his kingdom forever. I will be to him a father, and he shall be to me a son. When he commits iniquity, I will discipline him with the rod of men, with the stripes of the sons of men,

---

5. Wright, "A Christian Approach to Old Testament Prophecy Concerning Israel," 13.

but my steadfast love will not depart from him, as I took it from Saul, whom I put away from before you. And your house and your kingdom shall be made sure forever before me. Your throne shall be established forever.'" In accordance with all these words, and in accordance with all this vision, Nathan spoke to David.

Jesus is the faithful Davidic son who is given a kingdom that is eternal. But there's more. Jesus is the son of David *and* the son of Abraham. The significant promises to Abraham in Genesis 12 are expanded upon in the promises to David, and Jesus brings about the fulfillment of both.

There were already hints of this in the OT. Psalm 72, for example, is a "Messianic Psalm" that combines the promises of David and Abraham long before Matthew. There, Solomon spoke of a coming King whose rule would extend from "sea to sea" (Ps. 72:8, cf. Zech. 9:10), far beyond the borders of Israel. We read this about the coming King: "May people be blessed in him, all nations call him blessed" (Ps. 72:17). This "son of David" would be the King through whom all the nations of the earth would be blessed (Gen. 12:3, 18:18, 26:4).[6] This Davidic King will have the nations as His

---

6. "Indeed, it is being affirmed that a king in the line of David will be the means through which God's promise to bless the nations will be fulfilled. Those who stand to be blessed through Abraham here stand to be blessed through the Davidic king." Wright, *The Mission of God*, 345. Wellum writes, "The ultimate fulfillment of the Abrahamic covenant coincides with the ultimate fulfillment of the Davidic covenant. The Abrahamic blessings, linked back to Noah and creation, will only be ultimately realized through the Davidic son." "Baptism and the Relationship Between the Covenants" in *Believer's Baptism*, ed. Thomas R. Schreiner and Shawn D. Wright (Nashville: B&H Academic, 2006), 131.

heritage (Ps. 2:8). The offspring of the woman/Abraham/Judah is also the offspring of David. The hopes of Israel are coming to fruition in Jesus.

But this is no ordinary genealogy. For one, in the ancient world, women were not typically included in genealogies. We all know women are vital to the stuff of genealogies, but that was just how ancient folks recorded history. What is fascinating in this Jewish genealogy is that it includes women, but not those you'd expect. There is no mention of the Jewish matriarchs, instead you have a few shady ladies from Israel's history: Tamar, Rahab, Ruth, and "the wife of Uriah." And some are Gentiles —in the family record of the Jewish Messiah! Rahab was a Canaanite. Ruth was a Moabite. The law explicitly forbade Israelites from intermarrying with Moabites. Deuteronomy 23:3 reads, "No Ammonite or Moabite may enter the assembly of the LORD. Even to the tenth generation, none of them may enter the assembly of the LORD forever." Ammonites were the result of Lot's drunken incest. But here is a Moabite in the family record of Jesus. Then we have Bathsheba, who was presumably a Hittite like Uriah. The inclusion of these Gentiles would have been quite offensive to the average Jew, who referred to Gentiles as "dogs" and thanked the Lord daily "for not having made me a slave, a woman, or a Gentile."

The genealogy concludes with yet more emphasis on David:

> So all the generations from Abraham to David were

fourteen generations, and from David to the deportation to Babylon fourteen generations, and from the deportation to Babylon to the Christ fourteen generations. (Matt. 1:17)

What's with the number fourteen? Well, unlike English, Hebrew letters also represented numbers, and David's name without the vowels is DVD, which amounts to 4 + 6 + 4, which comes to 14. Again, Matthew is showing us that Jesus is the son of David. Here he alludes to the rise of David, the glory of David, the fall of David, and Israel is waiting for the coming King who will bring about the Kingdom. So verse 18 and following begins a new era, the new age of Israel, the age of her restoration.[7] Matthew is showing us that the coming of Jesus is the coming of God that puts an end to Israel's exile and overflows in blessing to the world.[8] As Richard Bauckham puts it, "For Matthew, Jesus is the Messiah not only for Jews but also for Gentiles. He is the descendant of Abraham through whom God's blessing will at last reach the nations."[9]

## GENTILE WORSHIPPERS FROM THE EAST

The well-known "Christmas" passages are actually all about

---

7. William J. Dumbrell, *The Search for Order* (Eugene, OR: Wipf and Stock Publishers, 2001), 157.
8. Roy E. Ciampa, "The History of Redemption," in *Central Themes in Biblical Theology* ed. Scott J. Hafemann and Paul R. House (Grand Rapids: Baker Academic, 2007), 292.
9. Richard Bauckham, *Bible and Mission* (Grand Rapids: Baker Academic, 2003), 33.

the restoration of Israel through Jesus and the Church. We sing the thesis of this book when we sing:

> *O come, O come, Emmanuel*
> *And ransom captive Israel*
> > *That mourns in lonely exile here*
> *Until the Son of God appear*
> > *Rejoice! Rejoice! Emmanuel*
> *Shall come to thee, O Israel.*

Rejoice! The Son of God has appeared to ransom Israel by ending her exile. In Matthew 2, we read of the visit of the "wise men from the east" (Matt. 2:1-12). They come to Jerusalem and ask where the King of the Jews was born. Overlooking the miracle of men stopping to ask for directions, let's examine the OT background for this visit. When Herod the pseudo-king (and all Jerusalem with him) hears of this, he gets nervous and asks of those who know the Bible where the Christ was to be born. They quote Micah 5:2, where we learn the King will be born in Bethlehem and will shepherd His people Israel (cf. 2 Sam. 5:2). The wise Gentile men found the child-King, worshipped Him, and gave Him gifts: gold, frankincense, and myrrh. Now, this would be a seemingly random story without the OT background. Doubtless, to many believers it is just that. As we will see again and again, when NT writers quote particular OT passages, they often have the larger context of that verse in mind as well. In Isaiah's prophecy of God returning to restore His people through a new exodus, he spoke of nations and kings coming and bringing their wealth with them (Isa. 60:5). "They shall bring gold and frankincense and shall bring good news, the praises of the Lord" (Isa. 60:6).[10] In Isaiah, they bring gifts to Zion, but in Matthew, they bring gifts to Jesus (Isa. 60:14). In line with what we saw from Isaiah 56 and 66, in Isaiah 60 we learn that foreigners will build up the walls of the temple and kings shall be priests (Isa. 60:10). Jesus is bringing about the fulfillment of Isaiah's vision, in His first coming. Gentile kings come to worship Israel's King.

## OUT OF EGYPT I CALLED MY SON

Next, let's look at Matthew 2:14-15: "And he rose and took the child and his mother by night and departed to Egypt and remained there until the death of Herod. This was to fulfill what the Lord had spoken by the prophet, 'Out of Egypt I called my son.'" Matthew quotes Hosea 11:1 here, and the context of the original quotation is important to grasp. There, Hosea recalls the first Exodus in the context of the prophecy of a coming new exodus (Hos. 11:5, 11). Matthew is picking up what Hosea was putting down. But now the Son of God is fleeing *into* Egypt, away from Jerusalem. The story of Jesus is the continuation and climax to the long story of Israel. Jesus is Israel, God's Son (Exod. 4:22), who is bringing about the new exodus as He redeems Israel from exile, not from Egypt,

---

10. For more on Isaiah 60 and the new creation, see Richard J. Mouw, *When the Kings Come Marching In: Isaiah and the New Jerusalem* (Grand Rapids: Eerdmans, 2002).

or from Rome, but from the real enemies who stand behind them: Satan, sin, and death.

## RACHEL'S WEEPING

Right after that, Matthew records how Herod killed all the male children in Bethlehem who were two years old and under. He says this was to fulfill what was spoken by Jeremiah:

> A voice was heard in Ramah, weeping and loud lamentation, Rachel weeping for her children; she refused to be comforted, because they are no more. (Matt. 2:18 quoting Jer. 31:15)

Again, keep in mind that NT authors often, if not always, have the larger context in mind. This is from the section of Jeremiah about the restoration of Israel and Judah (30:1-33:26). Ramah was just north of Jerusalem and on the way to Babylon (Jer. 40:1). So, though this particular verse is one of sadness due to Israel's exile, it is embedded in a larger context of hope for the end of exile. In fact, one is hard pressed to find a more hope-filled chapter for Israel than Jeremiah 31. "I have loved you with an everlasting love; therefore I have continued my faithfulness to you. Again I will build you, and you shall be built, O virgin Israel" (Jer. 31:3-4). The Lord will turn their mourning into joy (Jer. 31:13). Though Rachel, Israel's wife, is weeping from the grave for her children (Jer. 31:15), she should keep her voice from weeping and her eyes from tears for "there is hope" for their future, and they will come back to their own country (Jer. 31:16-17). Jeremiah 31 famously ends with the promise that God will make a new covenant with Israel and Judah where He will change them from the inside out and fully forgive their sins (Jer. 31:31-34). This chapter is about the end of Israel's misery. And Matthew wants us to see that Jesus is the agent of her redemption. He is the hope of Israel.[11]

ISRAEL THE NEW ASSYRIA?

In Matthew 3:1-12, we meet John the Baptist, who warns Israel not to take comfort in being biological children of Abraham because "God is able from these stones to raise up children for Abraham." Then he warns them that the axe is already laid to the root and trees that lack fruit will be cut down and burned. What is subversively fascinating is that John is using language from Isaiah 10 where God is about to "chop down" Assyria. Israel is in danger of becoming a new Assyria.[12]

---

11. "Through Jesus, God was at work to bring his people's 'exile' to an end." Walker, *Jesus and the Holy City*, 44; With Matthew 2:15-18 in mind, Richard B. Hays writes, "By evoking just these prophecies in the infancy narrative, Matthew connects both the history and the future destiny of Israel to the figure of Jesus, and he hints that in Jesus – Emmanuel – the restoration of Israel is at hand. This suggests that Matthew is not merely looking for random Old Testament proof texts that Jesus might somehow fulfill; rather, he is thinking about the shape of Israel's story and linking Jesus' life with key passages that promise God's unbreakable redemptive love for his people" *Reading Backwards: Figural Christology and the Fourfold Gospel Witness* (Waco: Baylor University Press, 2014), 43.
12. Peter J. Leithart, *The Four* (Moscow, ID: Canon Press, 2010), 58

## JESUS, THE FAITHFUL ISRAEL

Matthew 4 presents Jesus as the true and faithful Israel. He is baptized and affirmed and then sent out by the Spirit into the wilderness, hair still dripping. Like Israel, He is tested for 40 days, but unlike Israel, He is faithful. In fact, He does what Israel should have done. Three times He quotes from the book of Deuteronomy right before beginning His ministry—not in Jerusalem—but in Galilee *of the Gentiles* (Matt. 4:12-17).

## FISHING FOR EXILES

Progressing along Matthew's story, we see Jesus call His followers "fishers of men" (Matt. 4:19). As with most of the NT, there is OT background for this too. The pattern is emerging. Jesus is not merely using fishing as a good analogy for soul winning. This verse is also about the end of exile for the people of Israel and the gathering in of the exiles. Jeremiah had prophesied of a coming day when God would restore Israel by bringing them back from all over the place (Jer. 16:14-21). There, God said, "Behold, I am sending for many fishers, declares the Lord, and they shall catch them" (Jer. 16:16). Through the ministry of the followers of Jesus, God is restoring Israel.[13] The expansion of the Church is the fulfillment of Israel's destiny.

---

13. Gentry and Wellum, *Kingdom Through Covenant*, 490.

## FAITH > ETHNICITY

In Matthew 8, Jesus commends a Gentile woman's faith and says, "with no one in Israel have I found such faith. I tell you, many will come from east and west and recline at table with Abraham, Isaac, and Jacob in the kingdom of heaven, while the sons of the kingdom will be thrown into the outer darkness. In that place there will be weeping and gnashing of teeth" (Matt. 8:10-12). In the new age that Jesus brought about, faith is what is determinative to be included within the people of God. How one responds to Jesus determines one's destiny. Those who reject Him will be thrown out. But here Jesus predicts that Gentiles from all over will come and eat with Abraham, Isaac, and Jacob. Because of Jesus, Gentiles will be included as part of the family of Abraham.

## THE RENEWED 12 TRIBES SENT

In Matthew 10, we see the importance of the number 12.[14] Israel's King recruits 12 followers. Jesus is reconstituting the twelve tribes around Himself and sending them out to restore Israel, to the Jew first and also to the Greek.[15] He sends His

---

14. G.B. Caird, *Jesus and the Jewish Nation* (London: The Athlone Press, 1965), 16.
15. James M. Scott writes, "Jesus gathered around himself a group of precisely twelve disciples who symbolized the eschatological regathering of the twelve tribes of Israel." "Jesus' Vision for the Restoration of Israel as the Basis for a Biblical theology of the New Testament," in *Biblical Theology: Retrospect and Prospect* ed. Scott J. Hafemann (Downers Grove, InterVarsity Press, 2002), 133; Ciampa, "The History of Redemption," 290; Wright writes, "The gospels, in telling the story of Jesus (including the fulfillment of Israel's long narrative and the remarkable claim that this is also the story of God in person), declare in a thousand ways that Israel is hereby transformed, through its Messiah, Jesus, into a new community, based on him but shaped by the Twelve, who he called as one of his initial great symbolic actions." *How God Became King* (New York: HarperOne, 2011), 196. Chris Wright calls

people to the Jews as sheep in the midst of wolves who will flog them in "their" synagogues (Matt. 10:16-17). In Matthew 11:14, Jesus said that John the Baptist "is Elijah who is to come" (Matt. 11:14). Recall that our last book of the OT concludes with a promise that God would send His messenger Elijah to come and prepare the way before the Lord comes to purify and restore His people Israel (Mal. 3:1, 4:5), but unfortunately the Jewish people call John demonic and accuse Jesus of being a glutton and a drunkard (Matt. 11:18-19, 17:10-13), which results in Jesus saying that the Gentile cities would have responded in repentance unlike the Jewish cities in which He ministered (Matt. 11:20-24, 12:38-42). When He heads to Jerusalem, one would think His people would receive Him warmly, but instead He tells His disciples that in Jerusalem He will "suffer many things from the elders and chief priests and scribes, and be killed" (Matt. 16:21, 20:17-19, 27:1). Tragic.

## PARABLES AGAINST UNREPENTANT ISRAEL

In Jesus' later parables, He has some stinging words for those Paul will later call "Israel according to the flesh" (1 Cor. 10:18, my translation). First, consider the parable of the tenant (Matt. 21:33-46). Israel was known as the vineyard of the Lord (Isa. 5), and Jesus uses this to show how corrupt Israel had become. He tells the story of a tenant who grew a vineyard and leased it to tenants. When the time came to

---

this "the intentional symbolism of the embryonic twelve tribes of a restored Israel." Wright, "A Christian Approach to Old Testament Prophecy Concerning Israel," 11; Pate, et al., *The Story of Israel*, 129-31.

get his fruit, the tenants beat, killed, and stoned the master's servants. The master sent more servants who shared the same fate. Then he sent his son, for surely they would respect his son. Nope. They threw him out of the vineyard and killed him. The picture is clear. The master is the Father, the tenants are Israel, the servants are the prophets, and the son is Jesus. Jesus concludes the parable with these sharp words: "Therefore I tell you, the kingdom of God will be taken away from you and given to a people producing its fruits" (Matt. 21:43). He came to His own people but His own people did not receive Him, but to all who did receive Him through faith He gave the right to become children of God who were not born of natural descent but of God (John 1:11-13). Though I reject the label "replacement theology," if the only book of the Bible we had was Matthew's Gospel, one could fairly come to that conclusion.[16] As we move forward, we will see that in light of the whole canon, "inclusion theology" or "fulfillment theology" is more apt than replacement theology. Israel is not being replaced but being purified, expanded, and reconstituted around her Messiah.[17]

## STRIKE THE SHEPHERD AND JESUS' SHEEP WILL BE SCATTERED

Toward the end of Zechariah, we read of a shepherd being

---

16. This teaching causes NT scholar Richard Hays to write, "Matthew (alongside the letter to the Hebrews) is the preeminent canonical voice of supersessionist Christian theology: the church *replaces* Israel." *The Moral Vision of the New Testament* (New York: HarperOne, 1996), 424.
17. Goheen, *A Light to the Nations*, 84; Wright, *The New Testament and the People of God*, 275-78.

struck and Israel being scattered. Many will perish but God would purify a remnant and "they will call upon my name and I will answer them. I will say, 'they are my people'; and they will say, 'The Lord is my God'" (Zech. 13:7-9). Toward the end of Matthew's Gospel, Jesus quotes this very passage to refer to *His* followers being scattered (Matt. 26:31). The Church fulfills Israel.

THE GREAT ANNOUNCEMENT AND THE GREAT COMMISSION

Finally, we have Matthew 28, "the command of the new covenant."[18] Stunningly, the leaders of Israel assembled together, formed a lie, and paid off the soldiers to spread the lie that Jesus' body had been stolen (Matt. 28:11-15). Jesus came to His own and His own did not receive Him, but His plan all along was to expand the borders of Israel, which we see clearly in Matthew's "Great Commission." The all-important OT background is often overlooked here as well. Jesus begins the great commission with a "great announcement": all authority in heaven and on earth has been given to me (Matt. 28:18). This language is taken straight out of one of the most popular verses of Jesus' day: Daniel 7:13-14. That famous passage reads,

> I saw in the night visions, and behold, with the clouds of heaven there came one like a son of man, and he came to the Ancient of Days and was presented before

---

18. Wright, *The Mission of God*, 354.

him. And to him was given dominion and glory and a kingdom, that all peoples, nations, and languages should serve him; his dominion is an everlasting dominion, which shall not pass away, and his kingdom one that shall not be destroyed.

Jesus uses the same words that are recorded in the Greek version of Daniel for "authority" (*exousia*) and "given" (*edothē*). Dominion (or authority) was given to this Son of Man, and all nations will serve Him in His everlasting kingdom. We will see this below, but what is often missed is that this is a vision from heaven's perspective, so the coming of the Son of Man is a coming from earth to heaven, from earth to the Ancient of Days. The fulfillment of Daniel's vision begins in the first coming of Jesus and His ascension.

The commission continues: "Go therefore and make disciples of all nations, baptizing them in the name of the Father and of the Son and of the Holy Spirit, teaching them to observe all that I have commanded you. And behold, I am with you always, to the end of the age." Go, *therefore*. Go, because Jesus, as the Son of Man that Daniel spoke of, has all authority. One author has spoken of this as the mission equation: "If there is one Lord to whom all people belong and owe their allegiance, the people of that Lord must promote this reality everywhere."[19] "All nations" are to be discipled, taught and baptized. The words "all nations" (*panta ta ethnē*)

---

19. John Dickson, *The Best Kept Secret of Christian Mission* (Grand Rapids: Zondervan, 2010), 31.

come straight from the promises to Abraham (Gen. 18:18, 22:18) and the vision of Daniel that all nations would serve the Son of Man (Dan. 7:14). The nations are included in the restoration of Israel and this begins with Jesus sending out His followers.

So the Gospel of Matthew begins and ends with good news for the nations. It also begins and ends with the presence of God. Remember that although the temple has been rebuilt, the glorious presence of the Lord had never returned to that temple. God's presence was still missing. In Matthew's story, after the Gentile-filled Jewish genealogy, the angel said that this Jesus is "Immanuel," God with us (Matt. 1:23). Now, after the commandment to disciple the nations, Jesus promises: "And behold I am with you always" (Matt. 28:20).

*4*

# The Gospel According to Mark

As with Matthew, though less direct, Mark also portrays the story of Jesus as the continuation and climax of Israel's story.

## MARK'S HIGH-VOLTAGE INTRODUCTION

The obvious place to start our journey is in Mark's prologue, and boy, is it rich! Mark's gospel biscuit has been triple-dipped in the syrup of the OT. So we have some background work to do before we jump in. We need to have three OT visions in mind before we even move past Mark 1:3.[1] It should be no surprise that Isaiah 40 is first.

Mark begins his story with these words: "The beginning of the gospel of Jesus Christ, the Son of God." We could unpack "Christ" and "Son of God" as well, but for the sake of space we'll just look at the background of the word "gospel."

---

1. Rikk E. Watts, "Mark" in *Commentary on the New Testament Use of the Old Testament*, ed. G.K. Beale and D.A. Carson (Grand Rapids: Baker Academic, 2007), 113-20.

For the Greek ear, "gospel" was an imperial term that was used when a new emperor came to power. But for Jewish ears, Isaiah's new exodus vision came to mind.[2] The vision starts with Isaiah comforting Jerusalem by saying that God is coming to reveal His glory. Then we read, "Go on up to a high mountain, O Zion, herald of good news; lift up your voice with strength, O Jerusalem, herald of good news; lift it up, fear not; say to the cities of Judah, 'Behold your God'!" The word for "good news" is the same root for the word "gospel" that Mark uses. For Isaiah, the good news, i.e. the gospel, was the announcement that God was coming back to Jerusalem to restore His people and be enthroned as king.[3] Isaiah 52:7 says, "How beautiful upon the mountains are the feet of him who brings good news, who publishes peace, who brings good news of happiness, who publishes salvation, who says to Zion, 'Your God reigns'." The gospel Mark is seeking to communicate is the good news that God is returning to restore His people by suffering as a servant and being enthroned as king.

The second crucial OT passage is Malachi 3:1-2, which reads, "Behold, I send my messenger, and he will prepare the way before me. And the Lord whom you seek will suddenly come to his temple; and the messenger of the covenant in whom you delight, behold, he is coming, says the LORD of

---

2. Joel Marcus, *The Way of the Lord: Christological Exegesis of the Old Testament in the Gospel of Mark*, (Louisville: Westminster/John Knox Press, 1992), 18-21.
3. So the Greek background and the Hebrew background aren't all that different after all! See N.T. Wright, *What Saint Paul Really Said* (Grand Rapids: Eerdmans, 1997), 40-44.

hosts. But who can endure the day of his coming, and who can stand when he appears?" A little later, Malachi tells us who this messenger is: "Behold, I will send you Elijah the prophet" (Mal. 4:5). As we have already seen, this preparatory prophet is John the Baptist. So before the Lord comes to restore, He will send His messenger to warn of judgment for those who do not respond in repentance, lest he "come and strike the land with a decree of utter destruction" (Mal. 4:6). The day of the Lord will include salvation and judgment.

Malachi 3 alludes back to another OT passage: the exodus narrative: "Behold, I send an angel before you to guard you on the way and to bring you to the place that I have prepared" (Exodus 23:20). After having redeemed His people from Egypt, God sends an angel (i.e. messenger – *aggelon* LXX) ahead of them as they enter the promised land. Malachi picks up on this allusion to show that another messenger is coming who will make the way for another exodus.

The third OT passage to consider before turning to Mark is Isaiah 40:3: "A voice cries: 'In the wilderness prepare the way of the LORD; make straight in the desert a highway for our God'." Again, this is the beginning of Isaiah's kingdom vision of God coming back to rescue His people, defeat their enemies, vicariously suffer, and reign once again. The way of the LORD in Isaiah is the way of Yahweh.

Now, with all that OT background in mind, we are ready to look at Mark's introduction:

> The beginning of the gospel of Jesus Christ, the Son

of God. As it is written in Isaiah the prophet, 'Behold, I send my messenger before your face, who will prepare your way, the voice of one crying in the wilderness: "Prepare the way of the Lord, make his paths straight"' (Mark 1:1–3).

Mark quotes Isaiah and Malachi (who quotes Exodus). Mark wants us to see clearly that the story of Jesus is the continuation and climax of the story of the OT. Mixed citation was common in Mark's time, but he only gives credit to Isaiah here because he frames his whole story in light of the new exodus kingdom vision of Isaiah.[4] Malachi spoke of a coming messenger, who, as with the first exodus (Exod. 23), would lead Israel out of exile. He would prepare the way of Yahweh who would come to purify and restore His people. That messenger is John the Baptist (Mark 1:4), and the Lord who comes is Jesus of Nazareth (Mark 1:7). Isaiah had prophesied of the return of God to restore His people and usher in His kingdom through a new exodus. The first coming of Jesus is the return of God that Isaiah spoke of. God *has* come. Immanuel.

## THE END-TIME GIFT OF THE SPIRIT

A major expectation in the OT was the pouring out of the Spirit in the last days. One of the ways God would come and restore His people would be by pouring out the Spirit on all

---

4. For a dissertation-level treatment of Mark in light of Isaiah, see Rikki E. Watts, *Isaiah's New Exodus in Mark* (Grand Rapids: Baker Academic, 1997).

of them. The fundamental reason Israel could not keep the Law was because they did not have the power of the Holy Spirit to enable them to obey. As John Reisinger likes to put it, "The Old Covenant carried a footnote that said, 'Batteries not included.'"[5] So in the last days, God would remedy this with the democratization of the Spirit. When God returned to redeem and restore Israel, He said, "I will pour water on the thirsty land, and streams on the dry ground; I will pour my Spirit upon your offspring, and my blessing on your descendants" (Isa. 44:3). In the days of the new covenant, God says,

> I will sprinkle clean water on you, and you shall be clean from all your uncleannesses, and from all your idols I will cleanse you. And I will give you a new heart, and a new spirit I will put within you. And I will remove the heart of stone from your flesh and give you a heart of flesh. And I will put my Spirit within you, and cause you to walk in my statutes and be careful to obey my rules. (Ezek. 36:25-27)

Fast-forwarding to Mark, John the Baptist says, "I have baptized you with water, but he will baptize you with the Holy Spirit" (Mark 1:8). Jesus is inaugurating the last days and God is restoring Israel through His ministry.

---

5. John G. Reisinger, *But I Say Unto You* (Frederick, MD: New Covenant Media, 2006), 14.

## GOD RETURNING THROUGH THE TORN SKIES

Mark's story continues as John baptizes Jesus. Mark records,

> And when he came up out of the water, immediately he saw the heavens being torn open and the Spirit descending on him like a dove. And a voice came from heaven, "You are my beloved Son; with you I am well pleased." (Mark 1:10-11)

This imagery of the sky being "torn" open as God comes in power is straight out of—wait for it—Isaiah's new exodus vision. In Isaiah 63-64, we see a prayer for mercy for Israel. Isaiah teaches Israel to pray for God to "return for the sake of your servants, the tribes of your heritage" (Isa. 63:17). Then he prays, "Oh that you would rend the heavens and come down, that the mountains might quake at your presence" (Isa. 64:1). Mark is telling us that this prayer is being answered in the new covenant by the Son and the Spirit.[6] The heavens have been rent; God is returning through Jesus; the long-awaited time of Israel's rescue has dawned.

## THE SPIRIT-ENDOWED SERVANT SENT TO RESTORE ISRAEL

The sky is torn and the Spirit descends on Jesus like a dove. Yet again, this is in fulfillment of Isaiah's prophecy. Isaiah

---

6. Hays writes, "The gospel, according to Mark, is God's answer to Isaiah's intercessory cry: the tearing of the heavens and the descent of the Spirit upon Jesus signify that God's eschatological work of deliverance is beginning," "The Canonical Matrix of the Gospels," 56.

promised a servant who would be endowed with the Spirit. Isaiah 42:1 says, "Behold my servant, whom I uphold, my chosen, in whom my soul delights; I have put my Spirit upon him; he will bring forth justice to the nations" (see also Isa. 11:1-2). Isaiah 61:1-3 reads,

> The Spirit of the Lord GOD is upon me, because the LORD has anointed me to bring good news to the poor; he has sent me to bind up the brokenhearted, to proclaim liberty to the captives, and the opening of the prison to those who are bound; to proclaim the year of the LORD's favor, and the day of vengeance of our God; to comfort all who mourn; to grant to those who mourn in Zion—to give them a beautiful headdress instead of ashes, the oil of gladness instead of mourning, the garment of praise instead of a faint spirit; that they may be called oaks of righteousness, the planting of the LORD, that he may be glorified.

This Spirit-anointed Servant would restore "those who mourn in Zion." Mark is telling us that the Spirit-anointed Servant is Jesus Christ.

In Mark 1:11, the Father says of Jesus: "You are my beloved Son; with you I am well pleased." "Beloved Son" alludes to Psalm 2. There, the Lord decrees to the coming Davidic King: "You are my Son; today I have begotten you. Ask of me, and I make the nations your heritage" (Ps. 2:7-8). The future Davidic King will not only rule over Israel, but "all nations" will be His inheritance. We saw this in Psalm 72, but this fact of the universal reign of the Davidic King is also seen in the Davidic covenant itself. After God promises David a son whose kingdom will be eternal, David responds in prayer: "And yet this was a small thing in your eyes, O Lord GOD. You have spoken also of your servant's house for a great while to come, and this is instruction for mankind, O Lord GOD" (2 Sam. 7:19). These promises to David, the King of Israel, are "instruction for mankind."[7] They will ultimately benefit all nations. Jesus is the Davidic King to whom the nations bow. Jesus is the *royal* servant.

The phrase "well pleased" in Mark 1:11 is from Isaiah's new exodus vision as well. "Behold my servant, whom I uphold, my chosen, in whom my soul delights" (Isaiah 42:1). Jesus is the servant with whom the Father is "well pleased." Then Jesus begins His ministry and, as we have seen, in line with Jeremiah's teaching on the ingathering of the scattered children of God, He sends His disciples to fish for men, to go and gather Israel back to their King (Mark 1:17). So Mark is like an obnoxious street preacher, banging his drum, insisting that John the Baptist is the Elijah-like messenger (Mal. 3:1) who prepares the way for God to return to rescue His people, and that Jesus is the Spirit-endowed servant who fulfills that promise and sends His people out as an extension of His

---

[7]. Walter C. Kaiser, Jr., "The Blessing of David: The Charter for Humanity," in *The Law and the Prophets* ed. John H. Skilton (Phillipsburg, NJ: Presbyterian and Reformed, 1974), 298-318; Gentry and Wellum, *Kingdom Through Covenant*, 399-400.

ministry to gather and restore His people after a time of purification.

## JESUS' REDEFINITION OF FAMILY

In Mark 3:31-35, we hear about a crowd telling Jesus that His family was looking for Him and He answers that His family consists of whoever "does the will of God" (Mark 3:35). Jesus' family transcends the merely biological.

## JESUS VS. JERUSALEM

Malachi had warned that the Lord would come to His temple to clean house since it had become corrupt:

> Behold, I send my messenger, and he will prepare the way before me. And the Lord whom you seek will suddenly come to his temple; and the messenger of the covenant in whom you delight, behold, he is coming, says the LORD of hosts. But who can endure the day of his coming, and who can stand when he appears? For he is like a refiner's fire and like fullers' soap. (Mal. 3:1-2)

The messenger would be sent ahead to proclaim that the Lord is coming to the temple and Israel had better be prepared.

## THE KING ON A COLT

On His way to Jerusalem, Jesus sends a couple of His followers to find a colt (Mark 11:2). This is not some random idea Jesus happened to have. He wasn't merely tired. He had Zechariah's prophecy in mind.

Zechariah 9 speaks of the Lord coming to judge Israel's enemies and of the coming King of Zion. The people of Israel are told to rejoice greatly and shout aloud because her king is coming. He is coming "humble and mounted on a donkey, on a colt, the foal of a donkey" (Zech. 9:9). As should be expected by now, the rule of this King will be more expansive than the borders of Israel. He will rule "from sea to sea" (Zech 9:10). This King will restore Israel "double." "On that day the Lord their God will save them, as the flock of his people" (Zech. 9:16). Jesus is this King who comes on a colt to purify and restore His people. Some of them got it, at least for the moment. They realized that Jesus is the Davidic King coming to do what God had long promised, so they sing Psalm 118, a song about the victorious King coming to the temple in celebration: "Blessed is the coming kingdom of our father David! Hosanna in the highest" (Mark 11:10). Sadly, their enthusiasm soon waned.

## THE FIGLESS FIG TREE, THE NEW TEMPLE, AND THE DEN OF ROBBERS

On the way back into Jerusalem, Jesus sees a fig tree that had no figs on it and says, "May no one ever eat fruit from you again" (Mark 11:14). I once heard a man teach that this is just a random inclusion to show that Jesus was frustrated at times. Um, not quite. Jesus sees Himself as a new Jeremiah warning unrepentant Israel. Right after cursing the fig tree,

He cleanses the temple, knocking over tables and scathing His unrepentant people with the words, "Is it not written, 'My house shall be called a house of prayer for all the nations'? But you have made it a den of robbers" (Mark 11:17). Here, Jesus alludes to two OT passages: Isaiah 56 and Jeremiah 7.[8]

Isaiah 56 promises the salvation of Israel *and of Gentiles who join themselves to the Lord.* Then it speaks of these foreigners becoming priests and ministering to the Lord as His servants (Isa. 56:6). The very next verse says, "My house shall be called a house of prayer for all peoples," which Jesus quotes.

Jeremiah 7 was Jeremiah's "temple sermon." The Lord had told Jeremiah to stand at the gate of the temple and to warn the people: "Amend your ways and your deeds" (Jer. 7:3). If they would repent, God would let them dwell in that place. Then the Lord asks,

> Has this house, which is called by my name, become a den of robbers in your eyes? Go now to my place that was in Shiloh, where I made my name dwell at first, and see what I did to it because of the evil of my people Israel. And now, because you have done all these things, declares the LORD, and when I spoke to you persistently you did not listen, and when I called you, you did not answer, therefore I will do to the house that is called by my name, and in which you trust, and to the place that I gave to you and to your fathers, as I did to Shiloh. And I will cast you out of my sight, as I cast

---

8. Hays, *Reading Backwards*, 6-12.

out all your kinsmen, all the offspring of Ephraim. (Jer. 7:11-15)

Shiloh was their previous sanctuary, which God judged through the Philistines (Ps. 78:60-64). The "robbers" are those who trust in the temple but offer corrupt worship. If the worshipers don't change their ways, God will once again destroy the temple.

So Jesus has a double message when He combines these two passages.[9] He picks up Isaiah to say that the vision of priestly foreigners is coming, but currently the temple and its leadership is corrupt and, like at Shiloh, it's on the verge of being destroyed. "Elijah" had come to warn them, but Israel had not amended their ways. So Jesus would destroy the temple and build a new one where the nations would gather, He Himself being the cornerstone.

This is why the very next episode in the story is a return to the fig tree. The fig tree is a symbol of idolatrous Israel, which has "withered away to its roots" (Mark 11:20). Jesus is alluding to Jeremiah's judgment oracle on unrepentant Judah, when "there are no grapes on the vine, nor figs on the fig tree; even the leaves are withered, and what I gave them has passed away from them" (Jer. 8:13, cf. Micah 7:1). The messenger had come before the great and terrible day of the Lord but the Jewish people did to him "whatever they pleased" (Mark 9:13). So the Lord would come and curse the land. The figless fig tree served as a sobering illustration. Mark sandwiches the

---

9. Ciampa, "The History of Redemption," 291.

enacted judgment on the temple in between the fig tree to make his point dramatically clear.

## THE OLD TEMPLE'S DAYS ARE NUMBERED

We now conclude our walk through Mark by looking at the controversial "Olivet Discourse" in Mark 13. Many interpreters view this chapter as Jesus' teaching about the end of the world, but I hope to show that this is actually about the judgment and restoration of Israel, which makes it relevant for our purposes.[10]

Before turning to it, we must clear some ground. First, consider audience relevance. Jesus is speaking to His disciples in the first century. The Bible was written *for* us but most of it was not written *to* us. The "you" found throughout the chapter is referring to the disciples Jesus was speaking to. Second, keep in mind the clear teaching of Mark 13:30, where Jesus says: "Truly, I say to you, this generation will not pass away until all these things take place." Jesus says that all He talked about in chapter 13 would take place during that generation, which is roughly 40 years. Finally, the OT must be kept in mind when interpreting this knotty chapter, as should be clear by now. With these three truths in mind, let's dive in.

Matthew's Gospel, being longer, includes a bit more detail

---

10. For further exposition, see R.T. France, *The Gospel of Mark*. NIGTC (Grand Rapids: Eerdmans, 2002), 497-546; Sam Storms, *Kingdom Come*, 229-81; N.T. Wright, *Jesus and the Victory of God* (Minneapolis: Fortress, 1996), 339-69; Thomas R. Hatina, "The Focus of Mark 13:24-27: The Parousia, or the Destruction of the Temple?" *Bulletin for Biblical Research* 6 (1996), 43-66.

than Mark's account of the Olivet Discourse. In Matthew's account, after Jesus has pronounced those bone-shivering woes to the Jewish leaders, he laments over the state of Jerusalem:

> O Jerusalem, Jerusalem, the city that kills the prophets and stones those who are sent to it! How often would I have gathered your children together as a hen gathers her brood under her wings, and you were not willing! See, your house is left to you desolate. For I tell you, you will not see me again, until you say, 'Blessed is he who comes in the name of the Lord.' (Matt. 23:37-39)

Jerusalem was in for judgment. Jesus says to Israel, "your" house is now desolate. As Amos said, "O house of Israel: Fallen, no more to rise, is the virgin Israel; forsaken on her land" (Amos 5:2). It was time for judgment to begin in the household of God. As Jeremiah had said, "Thus says the LORD of hosts: So will I break this people and this city, as one breaks a potter's vessel, so that it can never be mended" (Jer. 19:11).

Akin to the glory of the Lord leaving the temple in Ezekiel (Ezek. 10:18-19, 11:22-23), Jesus leaves the temple, and one of His disciples, probably Peter, comments on how wonderful the temple was. Jesus does not share his enthusiasm, saying, "Do you see these great buildings? There will not be left here one stone upon another that will not be thrown down" (Mark 13:2). Jesus is asked when this will happen, and Jesus teaches *them* what *they* can expect. There would be false teachers, wars, earthquakes, and famine. The Jewish unbelievers would deliver them over to councils, and they would be beaten in synagogues. When they see the abomination of desolation standing where he ought not to be, which refers to the Roman army desecrating the temple (Dan. 9:27, 11:31, 12:11, Luke 21:20, Matt. 24:15), the disciples who are in Judea should flee to the mountains. Clearly this is a local judgment, for at the final judgment all are in danger, not just those in Judea. On that day, the mountains will be no refuge from the wrath of God.

Then we read in Mark 13:24-27:

> But in those days, after that tribulation, the sun will be darkened, and the moon will not give its light, and the stars will be falling from heaven, and the powers in the heavens will be shaken. And then they will see the Son of Man coming in clouds with great power and glory. And then he will send out the angels and gather his elect from the four winds, from the ends of the earth to the ends of heaven.

Let's look at these verses line by line. After the tribulation *in those* days the sun and moon will be darkened, stars will fall, and the powers in the heavens will be shaken. Taken literally, this does sound like the end of the world. But these verses should not be taken *literally* but *literarily*. Jesus was employing a common literary convention of His day and the days before

Him, what we now refer to as "apocalyptic language." It is the use of exaggerated de-creation language to signal major political shifts.

The OT is full of the stuff. Notice the similar language used when various empires were defeated in space-time history:

- Isaiah 13:10 – "For the stars of the heavens and their constellations will not give their light; the sun will be dark at its rising, and the moon will not shed its light."

- Isaiah 34:4 – "All the host of heaven shall rot away, and the skies roll up like a scroll. All their host shall fall, as leaves fall from the vine, like leaves falling from the fig tree."

- Ezekiel 32:6-8 – "I will drench the land even to the mountains with your flowing blood, and the ravines will be full of you. When I blot you out, I will cover the heavens and make their stars dark; I will cover the sun with a cloud, and the moon shall not give its light. All the bright lights of heaven will I make dark over you, and put darkness on your land, declares the Lord GOD."

Many more passages could be listed, but you get the point.[11] These verses are referring to the downfalls of Babylon, Edom, and Egypt respectively. Clearly, in these cases the world did

---

11. E.g. see Isa. 24:1-6, 19-23, Joel 2:10, 30-31, 3:15-16, Hab. 3:6-11, Jer. 4:23-28, Amos 8:9, Zeph. 1:14-16, Mal. 4:1-5. See Caird, *Jesus and the Jewish Nation*, 17-22; G.K. Beale, *The Temple and the Church's Mission: A Biblical Theology of the Dwelling Place of God* (Downers Grove: InterVarsity Press, 2004), 212-16; Wright, *Jesus and the Victory of God*, 360-65.

not end. Were the prophets wrong? No, they were not referring to the end of the space-time universe. They were using de-creation language to describe these events because the change would be *that* significant; the world would never be the same. "The destruction of earthly kingdoms is portrayed in terms of a heavenly shaking."[12] The prophets found themselves reaching for terminology of cosmic disorder to describe how theologically significant the transition would be.

We still do this in a sense. For example, if in 200 years a man is reading the history of the NBA and comes across a sentence that says, "In the early 2000s, Shaq was known for his earth-shattering dunks," he would be missing the point if he turned to his wife and said, "Wow, honey, this fellow called Shaq used to shatter the globe when he dunked a basketball. I wonder how they managed to put it back together after the games?" It is figurative language. The "literalist" reader misses the intended point.

In Mark 13 and elsewhere, this kind of figurative language indicates the downfall of seemingly permanent political and social orders. Jesus, in prophetic form, is using this complex mixture of metaphors to describe a massive event that was about to happen: the center of Jerusalem was about to be reduced to rubble. Remember that for Jews, the temple was viewed as the center of the creation. The world *as it was* is coming to an end. The Jewish people would never be the

---

12. Storms, *Kingdom Come*, 265.

same again. Jesus is saying something big is about to happen. Something apocalyptic.

But what about the Son of Man coming in clouds (Mark 13:26)? *Surely*, this is referring to the second coming of Jesus, right? Not so fast. Again, as we have seen over and over, the OT is informing what Jesus is talking about. Any Jew in Jesus' day who heard "Son of Man coming" would immediately think of the book of Daniel, which was a first century favorite. Jesus is quoting from Daniel 7:13-14:

> I saw in the night visions, and behold, with the clouds of heaven there came one like a son of man, and he came to the Ancient of Days and was presented before him. And to him was given dominion and glory and a kingdom, that all peoples, nations, and languages should serve him; his dominion is an everlasting dominion, which shall not pass away, and his kingdom one that shall not be destroyed.

As mentioned above in our discussion of the Great Commission, this is a vision *from heaven*. The Son of Man "comes" *from* earth *to* the Ancient of Days. This is ascension, not descension. The Son of Man ascends to the Father and is given all authority so that all nations would serve Him forever. So Jesus is making quite a statement about himself. He is the one Daniel saw. He will be vindicated. He will be given a kingdom that will include all peoples.

But from the surrounding context we know this "coming"

will include judgment, which is why Jesus includes a reference to "clouds." The Lord coming on clouds is frequently used in the OT to refer to His coming in judgment. For example, Isaiah 19:1 says, "Behold, the LORD is riding on a swift cloud and comes to Egypt; and the idols of Egypt will tremble at his presence." Ezekiel 30:3 says, "For the day is near, the day of the LORD is near; it will be a day of clouds, a time of doom for the nations" (cf. Joel 2:2, Psa. 97:2-3). In the OT, God would often use pagan nations, like Babylon and Assyria, to judge and punish His wayward people, and that is what is happening here, just as He said He would in the curses of Deuteronomy 27-29, Leviticus 26, and Isaiah 6:11-13. Jesus, through the Roman army, will "come" and judge the temple. Its leadership and everyone else would know that He was right and Jerusalem was wrong.[13] "The Temple is dethroned. Jesus is enthroned."[14]

So what does all this have to do with the Church and Israel? Verse 27 says this Son of Man will send out His messengers (*aggelous*) and gather His elect from the four winds, and from the ends of the earth to the ends of heaven. This is "regathering" language from the OT promises of when God would return to rescue and unite His scattered people. Listen to the words of Deuteronomy 30:4-6:

---

13. Caird writes, "Here, as in the book of Daniel, from which the imagery is drawn, the coming of the Son of Man on the clouds of heaven was never conceived as a primitive form of space travel, but as a symbol for a mighty reversal of fortunes within history and at the national level." *Jesus and the Jewish Nation*, 20; R.T. France, *Divine Government: God's Kingship in the Gospel of Mark* (Vancouver: Regent College Publishing, 1990), 81.
14. Storms, *Kingdom Come*, 281.

> If your outcasts are in the uttermost parts of heaven, from there the LORD your God will gather you, and from there he will take you. And the LORD your God will bring you into the land that your fathers possessed, that you may possess it. And he will make you more prosperous and numerous than your fathers. And the LORD your God will circumcise your heart and the heart of your offspring, so that you will love the LORD your God with all your heart and with all your soul, that you may live.

Isaiah had spoken of that day as well: "In that day the Lord will extend his hand yet a second time to recover the remnant that remains of his people, from Assyria, from Egypt, from Pathros, from Cush, from Elam, from Shinar, from Hamath, and from the coastlands of the sea" (Isa. 11:11, cf. Isa 49:12, Hab. 2:5). Later God promised, "Fear not, for I am with you; I will bring your offspring from the east, and from the west I will gather you. I will say to the north, Give up, and to the south, Do not withhold; bring my sons from afar and my daughters from the end of the earth" (Isa. 43:5-6). Zechariah had promised this gathering and the inclusion of the Gentiles within the people of God:

> Up! Up! Flee from the land of the north, declares the LORD. For I have spread you abroad as the four winds of the heavens, declares the LORD. Up! Escape

to Zion, you who dwell with the daughter of Babylon. For thus said the LORD of hosts, after his glory sent me to the nations who plundered you, for he who touches you touches the apple of his eye: "Behold, I will shake my hand over them, and they shall become plunder for those who served them. Then you will know that the LORD of hosts has sent me. Sing and rejoice, O daughter of Zion, for behold, I come and I will dwell in your midst, declares the LORD. And many nations shall join themselves to the LORD in that day, and shall be my people. And I will dwell in your midst, and you shall know that the LORD of hosts has sent me to you. (Zech. 2:6-11)

Then Jesus says, "Truly, I say to you, this generation will not pass away until all these things take place" (Mark 13:30). Jesus was a prophet if there ever was one. A generation was considered 40 years, and right at 40 years after Jesus spoke these words, the Roman army sieged Jerusalem and destroyed the temple. Not one stone was left on another. When Jesus uses Rome to judge the temple, He sends out His messengers to tell of the good news. As the Church grows, the promises of a regathered and restored Israel are being fulfilled. So the expansion of the Church is the fulfillment of the promises to Israel.[15]

---

15. "Israel's story is retold so as to reach a devastating climax, in which the present Jerusalem regime will be judged, and the prophet and his followers vindicated. The covenant god will use the pagan forces to execute his judgment on his people, and a new people will be born, formed around the prophet himself." N.T. Wright, *Jesus and the Victory of God*, 325.

5

# The Gospel According to John

"John's one overarching purpose in writing his Gospel is to share that God himself was finally redeeming Israel from her exile."[1] John, like Matthew, is fairly harsh on the unbelieving descendants of Abraham. The term "Jews" is rare in the other Gospels, occurring only five or six times, but John uses it more than seventy times, usually in a negative sense.[2]

## ALL WHO RECEIVE JESUS BECOME ISRAEL

John 1:11-13 says,

> He came to his own, and his own people did not receive him. But to all who did receive him, who

---

1. Pate, et al., *The Story of Israel*, 281.
2. Hays, *Moral Vision*, 425. E.g. see John 5:16-18, 39-40, 45-47. Though I don't agree, Hays goes so far as to say, "This Gospel's approach to OT interpretation lends itself, therefore, all too readily to anti-Jewish and/or high-handedly supersessionist theologies," *Reading Backwards*, 102.

believed in his name, he gave the right to become children of God, who were born, ==not of blood nor of the will of the flesh nor of the will of man==, but of God.

Israel's Messiah came to Israel but they wanted nothing to do with Him. Others did come to Him, and He gave them the right to become "children of God," that is to become Israel. They were not Israelites by blood or by natural descent. God made them His people.[3]

Later, Jesus would explain that this new birth had been predicted in Ezekiel 36:25-27 when God promised to give Israel a new spirit and to cleanse them with water. Israel should have known it was coming. Jesus rebuked Nicodemus for not knowing about it (John 3:5, 10). John (and Jesus) saw this as promise for anyone who received Him, that is, for the Church.

## JESUS, THE NEW TEMPLE

The latter chapters of Ezekiel speak of the day when God would come again and dwell with Israel in a rebuilt temple. John sees this vision as fulfilled in Jesus, the true temple. John 1:14 says, "And the Word became flesh and dwelt among us." The word for dwelt (*eskēnōsen*) is literally "tabernacled." John 2:19-21 says, "Jesus answered them, 'Destroy this temple, and in three days I will raise it up.' The Jews then said, 'It has taken forty-six years to build this temple, and will you raise

---

[3]. "It is in Jesus, and in those who follow him, of whatever race, that Israel's destiny is to be fulfilled." France, "Old Testament Prophecy and the Future of Israel," 74.

it up in three days'? But he was speaking about the temple of his body."

Jesus is the new temple. He is the meeting place between God and man. He is where heaven and earth overlap. He is the presence of God on earth. So the Jerusalem temple, which was prefigured in the tabernacle and in some ways before that in the garden, pointed forward to Jesus Christ. But that's not all. Jesus then sends the Spirit to fill the Church, corporately and individually (1 Cor. 3:16, 6:19, 2 Cor. 6:16). So in this age, we are the temple. But, ultimately, the whole world will be the temple, the dwelling place of God (Rev. 21-22).

Jesus says He will raise up this temple "in three days." Why three days? Why not one? Because Jesus is the means of the judgment and restoration of Israel. He is referring to Hosea, the "death bed prophet" of Israel.

Israel and Judah are in for punishment, but we read this in Hosea 6:2: "After two days he will revive us; on the third day he will raise us up, that we may live before him." Judgment is not the last word. They will destroy the temple, but on the third day, the true Israel will be raised up and will reconstitute and revive Israel around Himself.[4] The Messiah represents

---

4. Scott, "Jesus' Vision for the Restoration of Israel," 140; France writes, "Hosea 6:1-6 is all about Israel's (abortive) hope of national 'resurrection'. Jesus could only apply it to himself if he saw himself as in some way the heir to Israel's hopes. 'The resurrection of Christ is the resurrection of Israel of which the prophets spoke." "Old Testament Prophecy and the Future of Israel," 68; Wright, "A Christian Approach to Old Testament Prophecy Concerning Israel," 12. Walker says, "Jesus has taken a verse which originally referred to the restoration or revival of Israel and applied it instead to himself as Israel's Messiah. Israel's destiny was integrally bound up with the destiny of her representative Messiah. As Dodd rightly concluded: 'the resurrection of Christ is the resurrection of Israel of which the prophets spoke'." *Jesus and the Holy City*, 285.

and embodies the people. He is Israel summed up who restores repentant Israel. The people of God in the OT viewed resurrection as an end-time event when God would restore all of them (Ezek. 37). Resurrection meant the end of exile and the realization of the promises of God. What was surprising was for their singular representative to be raised in the middle of history. Jesus is the first fruits (1 Cor. 15:23), the firstborn from the dead (Col. 1:18). As LaRondelle puts it, "Jesus *is* Israel, and in His resurrection Israel's restoration is accomplished."[5]

## NEITHER THIS MOUNTAIN NOR THAT ONE

Jesus moves the focus from the temple in Jerusalem to a focus on Himself. Remember the Samaritan woman? She was at the well in the heat of the day, avoiding the crowds who would come early to get water. She lived a life of shame. Then she meets Jesus. You have to keep in mind that the relationship between Jews and Samaritans was hostile. Samaritans were considered unclean half-breeds. Later in John's gospel the Jews ask Jesus, "Are we not right in saying that you are a Samaritan and have a demon" (John 8:48)?

As they talk, she wants to get in a theological debate. She

---

5. LaRondelle, *The Israel of God in Prophecy*, 68; Thompson, *The Acts of the Risen Lord Jesus*, 71-101; N.T. Wright notes that "Resurrection, in the world of second-Temple Judaism, was about *the restoration of Israel* on the one hand and *the newly embodied life of all YHWH's people* on the other, with close connections between the two; and that it was thought of as the great event that YHWH would accomplish at the very end of 'the present age', the event which would constitute the 'age to come'." *The Resurrection of the Son of God* (Minneapolis: Fortress Press, 2003), 205; Walker, *Jesus and the Holy City*, 45.

says that her Samaritan fathers say they should worship on Mount Gerizim but the Jews say true worship happens in Jerusalem.[6] Jesus responds,

> Woman, believe me, the hour is coming when neither on this mountain nor in Jerusalem will you worship the Father. You worship what you do not know; we worship what we know, for salvation is from the Jews. But the hour is coming, and is now here, when the true worshipers will worship the Father in spirit and truth, for the Father is seeking such people to worship him. God is spirit, and those who worship him must worship in spirit and truth." The woman said to him, "I know that Messiah is coming (he who is called Christ). When he comes, he will tell us all things." Jesus said to her, "I who speak to you am he." (John 4:21-26)

The hour is coming and is now here when neither ethnicity nor geography matters in worship. What matters is spirit and truth. Jerusalem is no longer set apart. It has no distinct future as the new age transcends old covenant limitations. The woman left her jar and went back into town to tell of this "prophet," and John points out that even though the majority of Jews reject Jesus, "many Samaritans from that town believed in him" (John 4:39). *Jesus the temple* is the mediator between God and sinful mankind, even for those so-called "half-breed" Samaritans.

---

6. John 4:14 alludes to Joel 3:18 which is about the restoration of the temple (Joel 3:1).

## JESUS AND HIS PEOPLE AGAINST THE WORLD

John's Gospel shows that Jesus made a distinction between ethnic Jews and His true people. For example, notice how Jesus speaks of the Law of Moses:

- John 8:17 – "In *your* Law it is written that the testimony of two people is true." (emphasis mine)

- John 10:34 – "Is it not written in *your* Law, 'I said, you are gods'? (emphasis mine)

Jesus even goes so far as to equate the Jews with the "world." John 15:18-21 says,

> If the world hates you, know that it has hated me before it hated you. If you were of the world, the world would love you as its own; but because you are not of the world, but I chose you out of the world, therefore the world hates you. Remember the word that I said to you: 'A servant is not greater than his master.' If they persecuted me, they will also persecute you. If they kept my word, they will also keep yours. But all these things they will do to you on account of my name, because they do not know him who sent me.

The "world" is the Jews, and His people are not of the "world." It is often assumed that the Romans were the main persecutors of the early Church. That day did come, but in NT times, the Jews were the main persecutors of Jesus and the Church (John 5:16, throughout Acts). "They do not know him who sent me." Earlier, Jesus said to the Jews, "You know neither me nor my Father" (John 8:19, 47). We know that by "the world" Jesus is talking about the Jews because of how He concludes that section: "But the word that is written in *their* Law must be fulfilled: 'They hated me without a cause'" (John 15:25, emphasis mine). Also, in John 16, Jesus says that "they" will put His people out of the synagogues, and "they" will kill them thinking they are offering service to God, and "they will do these things because they have not known the Father, nor me" (John 16:3).

In John 8, the Jews boast of having Abraham as their father, but Jesus said that if God were their father, they would love *Him*. Then Jesus boldly asserts that they are children of the serpent. "You are of your father the devil, and your will is to do your father's desires" (John 8:44). As we will see below in Galatians, to be a child of Abraham is not a matter of biological descent, but of love for Jesus.

## THE GOOD SHEPHERD WHO COMES TO RESCUE ISRAEL

A couple of chapters later, Jesus says that He is the "good shepherd" (John 10:11). Just as in John 8, Jesus is making a grand claim here, grander than is often noticed. We have to know the OT background for this shepherd imagery. Back in Ezekiel 34, the Lord told Ezekiel to prophesy against the shepherds of Israel. Much like in Jesus' day, the shepherds were self-focused rather than focused on the people, but God warned them that He would come and judge them and rescue His sheep. God says,

> For thus says the Lord GOD: Behold, I, I myself will search for my sheep and will seek them out. As a shepherd seeks out his flock when he is among his sheep that have been scattered, so will I seek out my sheep, and I will rescue them from all places where they have been scattered on a day of clouds and thick darkness. And I will bring them out from the peoples and gather them from the countries, and will bring them into their own land. And I will feed them on the mountains of Israel, by the ravines, and in all the inhabited places of the country. I will feed them with good pasture, and on the mountain heights of Israel shall be their grazing land. There they shall lie down in good grazing land, and on rich pasture they shall feed on the mountains of Israel. I myself will be the shepherd of my sheep, and I myself will make them lie down, declares the Lord GOD. I will seek the lost, and I will bring back the strayed, and I will bind up the injured, and I will strengthen the weak, and the fat and the strong I will destroy. I will feed them in justice.

Notice how more than ten times God tells the people of Israel that He Himself will come to rescue them. But then in verse 23, the subject shifts: "And I will set up over them one shepherd, my servant David, and he shall feed them: he shall feed them and be their shepherd." God says, "I will come,

I will come, I will come...*David* will come." But David has long been six feet under. Ezekiel is referring to the future David, the Messiah. A new Davidic King will come, and His coming will be *God* coming. Jesus says, I am David. I am God returning to rescue and shepherd My people. I am the Good Shepherd, and My sheep are those who respond to Me with faith and repentance. The sheep of Israel in Ezekiel 34 are the Church in John who follow their Good Shepherd. They are His "little flock" (Luke 12:32), which is a reshaped image of Israel (Isa 40:11, Jer. 31:10, Ezek. 34:12-14).[7] He will bring in ethnic Jews to be sure, but He also has "other sheep that are not of this fold" who will listen to Him and they will be one flock under one shepherd (John 10:16).[8] They are secure in His hands. Jesus says, "My Father, who has given them to me, is greater than all, and no one is able to snatch them out of the Father's hand. I and the Father are one" (John 10:30).[9]

## GATHERING THE SCATTERED PEOPLE OF ISRAEL

We mentioned John 11:51-52 earlier, but it is worth repeating. Speaking of the prophecy of Caiaphas, John writes:

> He did not say this of his own accord, but being high

---

[7]. LaRondelle, *The Israel of God in Prophecy*, 102; France, "Old Testament Prophecy and the Future of Israel," 69.
[8]. LaRondelle writes, "As the messianic Shepherd, Christ declares here that He was sent to fulfill Israel's covenant promises of the gathering of Israel. As the Messiah He came to gather Israel to Himself (see Matthew 12:30), but more than that, to gather the Gentiles to Himself (see John 12:32)." Ibid., 100.
[9]. Hays, *Reading Backwards*, 89.

priest that year he prophesied that Jesus would die for the nation, and not for the nation only, but also to gather into one the children of God who are scattered abroad.

Jesus would die for Israel, but not for Israel only; He would also die for the scattered children of God. Recall the programmatic verses of John 1: Jesus came to Israel but Israel did not receive Him. But to those who did receive Him, to them He gave the right to become the children of God (John 1:11-13). Jesus comes to restore and regather Israel, that is, all who receive their King.

## JESUS IS ISRAEL, THE TRUE VINE

Like in Matthew, Jesus sees Himself as the embodiment of faithful Israel. Israel was commonly called the vine or the vineyard of the Lord (Isa. 5:1-7, Hos. 10:1, Matt. 21:33-46). Psalm 80:8 says, "You brought a vine out of Egypt; you drove out the nations and planted it." Unlike unfaithful Israel, Jesus is "the true vine" (John 15:1). What Jesus is saying is that He is the true Israel, and that what matters is being a branch in Him that bears fruit.[10] Jesus says, "I am the vine; you are the branches. Whoever abides in me and I in him, he it is that bears much fruit, for apart from me you can do nothing." (John 15:5). Being "in Jesus" the true vine is what makes one part of Israel, part of the vine. As we will see when we move along, this theme of Jesus as true Israel will be vital

---

10. Storms, *Kingdom Come*, 25-26.

for understanding the relationship between the Church and Israel.

# 6

# The Gospel According to Luke

## JESUS CAME TO FULFILL

Luke begins his Gospel this way: "Inasmuch as many have undertaken to compile a narrative of the things that have been accomplished among us" (Luke 1:1). The word for "accomplished" is *peplērophorēmenōn*, which is a form of the word for "fulfilled" (*plēroō*). So here is how the NIV translates it: "Many have undertaken to draw up an account of the things that have been fulfilled among us." Luke wants to inform Theophilus and us about the things that the story of Jesus has fulfilled. Again, we see that the long story of Israel is being brought to its climax through Jesus, her Messiah.

## THE MARVELOUS MAGNIFICAT

The first chapters of Luke are full of the fulfillment of OT expectation. We'll just take a look at a few. In Mary's

Magnificat, she sings that the Lord has "shown strength with his arm" (Luke 1:51), which is an allusion to the new exodus of Isaiah's prophecy when he spoke comfort for Zion: "Awake, awake, put on strength, O arm of the LORD" (Isa. 51:9, cf. 51:5, Psa. 89:10, 98:1, 118:16). God was coming back to destroy Israel's enemies, to forgive their sins, and to dwell with His people. Mary knows that the baby in her womb is bringing about these hopes for Israel in His first coming. The baby born in the manger is redeeming Zion.

Toward the end of her song, Mary sings,

> He has helped his servant Israel, in remembrance of his mercy, as he spoke to our fathers, to Abraham and to his offspring forever.

Mary knows that the coming of Jesus is the "helping" or restoration of Israel. By using the phrase "servant," Mary is again recalling the new exodus vision of Isaiah (see Isa. 41:8-9, 44:21, 49:3). God will be faithful to act on Israel's behalf because He made a promise to Abraham. The coming of Jesus is fulfilling the promise to Abraham and His offspring and the vision of God coming to renew and restore Israel.

### ZECHARIAH'S PROPHECY

After the birth of John the Baptist, Zechariah is filled with the Spirit and prophesied, saying,

> Blessed be the Lord God of Israel, for he has visited

and redeemed his people and has raised up a horn of salvation for us in the house of his servant David, as he spoke b the mouth of his holy prophets from of old, that we should be saved from our enemies and from the hand of all who hate us; to show the mercy promised to our fathers and to remember his holy covenant, the oath that he swore to our father Abraham, to grant us that we, being delivered from the hand of our enemies, might serve him without fear, in holiness and righteousness before him all our days. And you, child, will be called the prophet of the Most High; for you will go before the Lord to prepare his ways, to give knowledge of salvation to his people in the forgiveness of their sins, because of the tender mercy of our God, whereby the sunrise shall visit us from on high to give light to those who sit in darkness and in the shadow of death, to guide our feet into the way of peace. (Luke 1:68-79)

This prophecy is plumb full of promises about the hope of Israel: the God of Israel has visited and redeemed Israel by sending the Davidic son "as he spoke by the mouth of his holy prophets from of old" (Luke 1:70). He did this so Israel could be saved, and so the God of Israel could show mercy that He promised to the fathers and to remember His covenant with Abraham. He says that His son will be the long awaited messenger who will "give knowledge of salvation to his people" (Luke 1:77). Zechariah is rejoicing that all these promises are coming to fruition in his own day! Jesus is bringing about the salvation of Israel in His first coming. Christmas is about the end of exile for the people of God.

## SIMEON SEES ISRAEL'S CONSOLATION

When baby Jesus is presented at the temple for purification, Simeon was expecting Him. He was a devout Jew "waiting for the consolation of Israel" (Luke 2:25). The word for "consolation" (*paraklēsin*) can also be translated "comfort." Remember that the opening verses of Isaiah's new exodus vision about the end of Israel's exile begins with "comfort, comfort [*parakaleite*] my people" (Isa. 40:1, cf. 49:13, 51:3, 57:18, 61:2). Simeon knew his Bible. He had reflected on the grand promises of God, and the Spirit had revealed to him that he would be alive when the kingdom of God was ushered in. He would not see death "before he had seen the Lord's Christ" (Luke 2:26). He would see the Messiah. He would see God begin to fulfill His saving promises. When Jesus was brought in, Simeon sweeps Him up and praises the Lord for letting him see his great salvation:

> Lord, now you are letting your servant depart in peace, according to your word; for my eyes have seen your salvation that you have prepared in the presence of all peoples, a light for revelation to the Gentiles, and for glory to your people Israel. (Luke 2:29-32)

Simeon alludes to Isaiah two more times here. "My eyes have seen your salvation" is from Isaiah 52:10: "the ends of the earth shall see the salvation of our God." "A light for revelation to the Gentiles" is from Isaiah 49, which we have seen is about the Servant of the Lord who will sum up Israel and restore her. The Lord will make this Servant "a light for the nations, that my salvation may reach to the end of the earth" (Isa. 49:6, cf. 42:6, 60:3). God will save the nations through the restored people of God. Simeon knew that the Christ child would become this "light of the world" (cf. John 8:12).

He will be a light to the Gentiles and a light for glory "to your people Israel" (Luke 2:32). The story of Jesus is the story of the climax of Israel and the fulfillment of her hopes. Again, Simeon has Isaiah in the back of his mind: "In the LORD all the offspring of Israel shall be justified and shall glory" (Isa. 45:25). "I bring near my righteousness; it is not far off, and my salvation will not delay; I will put salvation in Zion, for Israel my glory" (Isa. 46:13). Simeon rightly sees that Jesus is coming to bring these hopes about. Then he tells Mary, "Behold, this child is appointed for the fall and rising of many in Israel" (Luke 2:34). Simeon knows that the dawning of the kingdom will have a dark side (Luke 12:49-53).[1] Israel is being saved, but saved through judgment.

Simeon was not the only faithful Jew eagerly waiting Israel's redemption. Toward the end of Luke's Gospel, we meet Joseph of Arimathea who "was looking for the kingdom of God" (Luke 23:51). Jesus, by His bloody death, ushers

---

1. Goheen, *A Light to the Nations*, 83.

in the new covenant/new exodus/salvation of Israel/ redemption/Kingdom.

## 84-YEAR-OLD ANNA OF ASHER

Next we have an interesting little tidbit for Luke to include in his Gospel. He mentions an old faithful prophetess named Anna who was always at the temple. When Jesus was being presented there, she comes up, gives thanks to God, and tells everyone who was "waiting for the redemption of Jerusalem" about this Christ-child (Luke 2:38). Luke wants to be clear: Jesus is restoring Israel.

## GRACE FOR THE ENEMIES?

Then Luke shows us that this coming Kingdom will include more than just Israel. It is international in scope. Jesus goes to the synagogue on the Sabbath and opens the Isaiah scroll to Isaiah 61 and reads from it:

> The Spirit of the Lord is upon me, because he has anointed me to proclaim good news to the poor. He has sent me to proclaim liberty to the captives and recovering of sight to the blind, to set at liberty those who are oppressed, to proclaim the year of the Lord's favor. (Luke 4:18-19)

Then He rolls up the scroll, sits down, and with all eyes on the local carpenter, He says, "Today this Scripture has been fulfilled in your hearing." Just imagine the scenario: a local

30-year-old man walked into a meeting in a hill town called Nazareth and announced that the time had come for God to return, and guess what...He's here! Talk about a mic drop if ever there was one. Jesus just said that He is the Spirit-endowed Servant who will bring about the hopes of Israel. Incredible.

At first, the audience is intrigued, but Jesus knows better. He knows this same group will end up rejecting Him. Then He retells a few familiar Bible stories. To say the least, they didn't warm His hearers' hearts. Jesus reminds the people of times when God sent prophets to His people, but they were rejected so He sent them elsewhere. He reminds them of the time that Elijah was sent to a *Gentile* widow in Sidon during the famine when there were many Jewish women in need as well. Then He reminds them of the time that Elisha was sent to cleanse Naaman, the commander of the enemy army of Syria, from his leprosy, even though there "were many lepers in Israel" (Luke 4:27). Jesus proclaims that the restoration of Israel which Isaiah spoke about is here in Him and that it will look different than they expected.[2] "Outsiders" will benefit, too. And rather than being excited as they should have been, they seek to throw their Spirit-endowed Servant off a cliff!

### TAX COLLECTORS INCLUDED?

We often breeze over the call of Levi without reflecting on

---

2. "Jesus clearly understood his own mission in terms of the fulfillment of the prophetic hope of the restoration of Israel. This was no longer something future, but a present reality through the arrival of the kingdom of God in his own person." Wright, "A Christian Approach to Old Testament Prophecy Concerning Israel," 9.

just how crazy it is in its first century context. Remember that tax collectors were hated by the Jewish people. They even believed it was righteous to lie to tax collectors. That's one of the Big Ten.

Tax collectors were enemies of the people of God because they turned on them, went to work for the enemy, and then robbed from the poor to pad their pockets. Most Jews were waiting on their Messiah to come and destroy such blaspheming idolaters, but Jesus comes and calls them to Himself, then parties with them. The Jewish leaders grumble over this, and Jesus tells them why He came: "Those who are well have no need of a physician, but those who are sick. I have not come to call the righteous but sinners to repentance" (Luke 5:31-32).

A couple of chapters later, Luke records the story of a "woman of the city" coming to serve Jesus (Luke 7:36-50). The Pharisee looks down on Him for allowing this woman to touch Him, but Jesus uses the woman to teach this Jewish leader a thing about who truly worships God. The "wrong" people are entering the kingdom while the "right" people miss it.

## ARE YOU THE ONE WHO IS TO COME?

In Luke 7, John the Baptist's people come to Jesus and ask if He really is the one to bring about the new covenant and new exodus spoken of by the prophets? Apparently, John was expecting something else as well. Jesus tells them to go tell John what they have seen and heard. He then quotes Isaiah

35, where Isaiah envisions new creation: the wilderness will be glad and the desert shall rejoice and blossom. Be strong for God is coming and will save you (Isa. 35:4). Isaiah 35:5-6 reads,

> Then the eyes of the blind shall be opened, and the ears of the deaf unstopped; then shall the lame man leap like a deer, and the tongue of the mute sing for joy. For waters break forth in the wilderness, and streams in the desert.

Keeping in mind that Jesus often had the broader OT context in mind when quoting or alluding to the Hebrew Scriptures, we should note that Isaiah 35:10 says, "The ransomed of the LORD shall return and come to Zion with singing." Though it doesn't look like what many Jews expected, Jesus is bringing about the restoration of Zion.

## THE ONE TO REDEEM ISRAEL

In the last chapter of Luke's story, we learn about a couple of frowning Jews walking to Emmaus. They were disappointed. The one who they had hoped was the Messiah was crucified by their own people (Luke 24:20). They told Jesus, "We had hoped he was the one to redeem Israel" (Luke 24:21). By this point in the story, Luke has made it clear that Jesus is redeeming Israel, just as the prophets had foretold. Jesus rebukes them, saying, "O foolish ones, and slow of heart to believe all that the prophets have spoken! Was it not necessary that the Christ should suffer these things and enter into his glory" (Luke 24:25-26)? Jesus then gives them a lesson in OT Hermeneutics 101, interpreting the Law and the Prophets in light of Himself. Turns out, their hopes were right: Jesus is the one to redeem Israel.

Before ascending to the Father, He tells His disciples,

> "These are my words that I spoke to you while I was still with you, that everything written about me in the Law of Moses and the Prophets and the Psalms must be fulfilled." Then he opened their minds to understand the Scriptures, and said to them, "Thus it is written, that the Christ should suffer and on the third day rise from the dead, and that repentance and forgiveness of sins should be proclaimed in his name to all nations, beginning from Jerusalem. You are witnesses of these things. And behold, I am sending the promise of my Father upon you. But stay in the city until you are clothed with power from on high." (Luke 24:44-49)

The OT Scriptures are about Jesus, and they cannot be rightly grasped until one sees this. As the Law and Prophets foretold, the Servant would die and rise, and this good news must be announced to all nations. The disciples are "witnesses" of these things, and the Spirit-endowed Servant will become the Spirit-bestowing Servant. They will be clothed with power from on high, which is a quotation of Isaiah 32:15, where the pouring out of the Spirit from on high will result in the new creation, i.e. the kingdom. This matrix of Spirit, power, kingdom, and witness points forward to the first chapter of Luke's second volume. To that we now turn.

# 7

# Acts

As with so much of the NT, the book of Acts is also soaked with the "fifth gospel" of the canon of Scripture: Isaiah. Like Mark, the book of Acts is informed at every step by Isaiah's new exodus vision.[1]

## RESTORING THE KINGDOM TO ISRAEL

Acts 1 is a key passage in the Church/Israel discussion. The resurrected Jesus appeared to His disciples and spoke about the kingdom of God for forty days and tells them to wait in Jerusalem for the gift of the Holy Spirit. The disciples then ask Jesus, "Will you at this time restore the kingdom to Israel" (Acts 1:6)? Jesus responds:

---

1. David Pao identifies six interrelated themes tied to the restoration of Israel in Isaiah's new exodus program: ingathering of exiles, community of the spirit, rebuilding of the Davidic Kingdom, repentance, and the inclusion of outcasts, *Acts and the Isaianic New Exodus* (Grand Rapids: Baker Academic, 2000), 112-21.

> It is not for you to know times or seasons that the Father has fixed by his own authority. But you will receive power when the Holy Spirit has come upon you, and you will be my witnesses in Jerusalem and in all Judea and Samaria, and to the end of the earth.

Jesus refuses to give them a precise timetable, but the answer to the question is yes, just not in line with their expectations.[2] He was not changing the subject.[3] We know this from what Jesus says and the way He echoes the kingdom vision of Isaiah.

Let's break it down phrase by phrase. We saw at the end of Luke's first volume that Jesus' disciples were to wait to receive "power from on high," which alludes to Isaiah 32:15. The power is the Holy Spirit, who will "come upon you." Here, Jesus has Isaiah 44:3-5 in mind:

> For I will pour water on the thirsty land, and streams on the dry ground; I will pour my Spirit upon your offspring, and my blessing on your descendants. They shall spring up among the grass like willows by flowing

---

2. O. Palmer Robertson, *The Israel of God* (Phillipsburg, NJ: P&R, 2000), 127-37; Storms, *Kingdom Come*, 284-88. Thompson, *The Acts of the Risen Lord Jesus*, 45, 46, 104-08, 114, 127. As Tom Wright notes, "Jesus' answer is usually taken as a 'not yet': 'it is not for you to know times or seasons.' Yet Luke surely intended us to read it as a 'yes, but not in that way': 'You will receive power, when the Holy Spirit comes upon you and you will be my witnesses. . . to the end of the world" "Jerusalem in the New Testament" in P.W.L. Walker, *Jerusalem Past and Present in the Purposes of God* (Cambridge: Tyndale House, 1992), 68; Walker, *Jesus and the Holy City*, 292.
3. Russell D. Moore, *The Kingdom of Christ* (Wheaton: Crossway, 2004), 119.

streams. This one will say, 'I am the LORD's,' another will call on the name of Jacob, and another will write on his hand, 'The LORD's,' and name himself by the name of Israel.

The phrase "you will be my witnesses" also has an Isaianic background. Isaiah 43:12 says, "I declared and saved and proclaimed, when there was no strange god among you; and you are my witnesses," declares the LORD, "and I am God" (cf. Isa. 44:8). "To the ends of the earth" is from Isaiah 49:6 where the Servant of the Lord (Messiah) will restore the servant of the Lord (Israel). God will make this renewed people to do what original Israel was supposed to be: "I will make you as a light for the nations, that my salvation may reach to the end of the earth." Luke already used Isaiah 49:6 at the end of his first volume when describing the early Church's mission. They would witness to the gospel and "repentance and forgiveness of sins should be proclaimed in his name to all nations, beginning from Jerusalem" (Luke 24:47).

So Jesus' response is all about the kingdom. His every phrase is full of echoes of Isaiah's vision of the kingdom. Jesus is restoring the kingdom to Israel, and He is doing so *through* His people.[4] The disciples ask Jesus, "When will *You* restore

---

4. As Robertson puts it, "The kingdom of God would be restored to Israel in the rule of the Messiah, which would be realized by the working of the Holy Spirit through the disciples of Christ as they extended their witness to the ends of the earth," *The Israel of God*, 134. Thompson writes, "Thus, in his reply to the disciples, Jesus does not reject their enquiry into God's promises of restoration, whether in redirecting this hope to a distant future or in rebuking a nationalistic focus. He is, rather, affirming

the kingdom," and Jesus says, "I will do it through *you* as my witnesses." This is why Luke begins his second volume by telling Theophilus that the first book was about all that Jesus *began* to do and teach (Acts 1:1). Volume two is still about what Jesus is doing—only now He is doing it through the Church, through the reconstituted Twelve, which is why one of the first orders of business is to replace Judas with Matthias to get back to twelve rather than eleven (Acts 1:12-26, 26:7).[5] This is what the book of Acts is all about: the reconstitution and restoration of the kingdom to Israel-reshaped-around-Messiah.[6] So the rest of the book of Acts fills out the answer to the question posed in Acts 1:8.

## TIMES OF REFRESHING

I will say more about the Spirit and the Church below, but here I just mention that Pentecost (Acts 2) is key to the

---

and clarifying their role in this restoration. As God has promised, this restoration will involve the enabling of God's Holy Spirit, the transformation of God's people who bear witness to the Saviour, and the inclusion of the nations." *The Acts of the Risen Lord Jesus*, 108; Wright agrees: "Jesus thus commissions his disciples to be witnesses to a restoration of Israel with worldwide effects, fully in line with the Isaianic eschatology." Wright, "A Christian Approach to Old Testament Prophecy Concerning Israel," 12.

5. Goheen, *A Light to the Nations*, 84. Gerhard Lohfink writes, "The Twelve are chosen out of a much larger number of disciples. They represent the twelve tribes; they are the beginning and center of growth for the renewed, eschatological Israel. All discipleship is thus aimed at Israel and at the gathering of the whole people of God. With the disciples begins the eschatological re-creation of Israel, and in the re-creation of Israel the reign of God is revealed." *Does God Need the Church? Toward a Theology of the People of God*, trans. Linda M. Maloney (Collegeville, MJ: Liturgical Press, 1999), 131.

6. Pao persuasively argues that the reference to Jerusalem, Judea, Samaria, and the ends of the earth is a reference to one city, two regions, and the Gentiles. The two regions, Judea and Samaria, refer to the reunification of the N and S kingdoms. So Acts 8:1, 14, 9:31, *Acts and the Isaianic New Exodus*, 91-96.

difference between Israel and the Church. In Acts 3, Peter is preaching in Solomon's portico and says,

> Repent therefore, and turn back, that your sins may be blotted out, that times of refreshing may come from the presence of the Lord, and that he may send the Christ appointed for you, Jesus, whom heaven must receive until the time for restoring all the things about which God spoke by the mouth of his holy prophets long ago. Moses said, 'The Lord God will raise up for you a prophet like me from your brothers. You shall listen to him in whatever he tells you. And it shall be that every soul who does not listen to that prophet shall be destroyed from the people.' And all the prophets who have spoken, from Samuel and those who came after him, also proclaimed these days. You are the sons of the prophets and of the covenant that God made with your fathers, saying to Abraham, 'And in your offspring shall all the families of the earth be blessed.' God, having raised up his servant, sent him to you first, to bless you by turning every one of you from your wickedness. (Acts 3:19-26)

Peter tells his fellow Jews that Jesus has ascended and that the restoration predicted by the prophets is now in process (*arxi*). Moses had prophesied of a coming prophet that his people should listen to (Deut. 18:15-18) and "it shall be that every soul who does not listen to that prophet shall be destroyed from the people" (Acts 3:23). Peter then reminds them that they are sons of the covenant made with Abraham and that their very existence was so "all the families of the earth" would be blessed. Now God has raised up His "servant" and sent Him to the Jews first. If Israel is to be a light to the nations, they must first have their darkness removed. Peter, too, had Isaiah 49 in mind. Isaiah 49:5-6 reads,

> And now the LORD says, he who formed me from the womb to be his servant, to bring Jacob back to him; and that Israel might be gathered to him— for I am honored in the eyes of the LORD, and my God has become my strength— he says: "It is too light a thing that you should be my servant to raise up the tribes of Jacob and to bring back the preserved of Israel; I will make you as a light for the nations, that my salvation may reach to the end of the earth."

The Servant would come to restore Israel, to bring Jacob back, to gather Israel, and to raise up the tribes of Jacob so they can at last become a light for the nations. The calling of Israel was always for the salvation of the nations. They turned inward, but God would come to remake an effective, outward looking Israel. This is what Acts is about. The kingdom program of Isaiah, indeed "all the things about which God spoke by the mouth of his holy prophets" is beginning to be fulfilled through the Church in the first century.

## THE ETHIOPIAN EUNUCH

In Acts 8, Philip is sent south and meets an Ethiopian eunuch who worked for the queen. This was a Gentile who worshiped the God of Israel, even though Deuteronomy 23 declared that no one whose male organ is cut off could enter the assembly of the LORD. As you might imagine by now, he was reading the prophet Isaiah. Chapter 53, in fact! As in every evangelist's dream, he asks Philip to help him understand. He was reading about the Servant who was sacrificed for His people. Philip begins there and tells him the gospel of Jesus. The eunuch believes and is baptized. What does this have to do with the Church and Israel? Why, more OT background is needed, of course. Remember the vision of Isaiah 56:

> Let not the foreigner who has joined himself to the LORD say, "The LORD will surely separate me from his people"; and let not the eunuch say, "Behold, I am a dry tree." For thus says the LORD: "To the eunuchs who keep my Sabbaths, who choose the things that please me and hold fast my covenant, I will give in my house and within my walls a monument and a name better than sons and daughters; I will give them an everlasting name that shall not be cut off. "And the foreigners who join themselves to the LORD, to minister to him, to love the name of the LORD, and to be his servants, everyone who keeps the Sabbath and does not profane it, and holds fast my covenant— these I will bring to my holy

mountain, and make them joyful in my house of prayer; their burnt offerings and their sacrifices will be accepted on my altar; for my house shall be called a house of prayer for all peoples." The Lord GOD, who gathers the outcasts of Israel, declares, "I will gather yet others to him besides those already gathered." (Isa. 56:3–8)

When the kingdom comes, the foreigners and eunuchs would be included within the people of Israel. Their lot would be "better than sons and daughters." So the salvation of the eunuch is Luke showing us again that the kingdom Isaiah foresaw is unfolding in the ministry of the early Church.

### LIGHT FOR THE NATIONS

When the Jews became jealous and contradicted the gospel that Paul and Barnabas were preaching, they say,

> It was necessary that the word of God be spoken first to you. Since you thrust it aside and judge yourselves unworthy of eternal life, behold, we are turning to the Gentiles. For so the Lord has commanded us, saying, 'I have made you a light for the Gentiles, that you may bring salvation to the ends of the earth'. (Acts 13:46-47)

Isaiah 49 again! Here Paul and Barnabas refer to *themselves* as the light for the nations. But I thought that was talking about Jesus (Luke 2:32, cf. Acts 26:23)? Remember that Isaiah 49 speaks of the servant Israel who will restore the servant

Israel. So is the servant of Isaiah 49 about Jesus or the Church? Yes.[7] This is a perfectly Jewish way of viewing things. Jesus is the servant who restores the servant Israel. And there is an organic connection between the head and the body. Jesus is bringing about the salvation of Israel; Jesus' body is bringing about the salvation of Israel. The Messiah is a "corporate personality." Israel had dropped the ball on their calling to be a light to the nations.[8] Jesus comes and faithfully embodies Israel as "light of the world" (John 8:12) and redeems His renewed people to be "light of the world" (Matt. 5:14). The early Church knew that her mission was the restoration of Israel.

In Paul's defense before Agrippa, he said that he was on trial "because of my hope in the promise made by God to our fathers, to which our twelve tribes hope to attain" (Acts 26:6-7). His mission is fulfilling the Abrahamic promise and the hope of the twelve tribes. In the last chapter of Acts, Paul tells the Jewish leaders that he is imprisoned because of the "hope of Israel" (Acts 28:20). Israel is being rescued and reconstituted through the expansion of the Church.

## THE REBUILDING OF DAVID'S FALLEN TENT

In Acts 15, we learn about the Jerusalem Council. Some Jews were teaching Christians that they must be circumcised to be

---

7. Thompson, *The Acts of the Risen Lord Jesus*, 119; LaRondelle, *The Israel of God in Prophecy*, 107-08. I. Howard Marshall, "Acts," in *Commentary on the New Testament Use of the Old Testament*, 588; Wright, *The Mission of God*, 519-21.
8. Jonah is a nice picture of the people of Israel as a whole. He knows he is called to be a "light to the nations" but is so ethnocentric that he heads the opposite direction because God will give grace to the pagans.

saved, so Paul and Barnabas met with the leaders in Jerusalem. The elders and apostles hashed it out, and Peter, Paul, and Barnabas explained how God had been at work among the Gentiles. Their leader, James, responds and agrees with Peter and Paul, saying that this inclusion of the Gentiles within the people (*laos*) of God was foretold in the prophets. He cites Amos 9:11-12:

> After this I will return, and I will rebuild the tent of David that has fallen; I will rebuild its ruins, and I will restore it, that the remnant of mankind may seek the Lord, and all the Gentiles who are called by my name, says the Lord, who makes these things known from of old.' (Acts 15:16-17)

Amos is largely about the pending judgment of Israel for their idolatry and mistreatment of the poor. As the Minor Prophets often do, Amos speaks of the restoration of Israel after the judgment. This is the section James quotes from.

Amos 9:11-15 is about the restoration of Israel. It is about the raising up of the fallen booth of David (Amos 9:11). It is about the restoring of "the fortunes of my people Israel" (Amos 9:14). James sees the salvation of Gentiles and quotes *this verse* to speak of *that reality*. Don't miss this! He does not apply this passage to some future millennial kingdom.[9] At a council of the Church where the point of the meeting

---

9. Benjamin L. Merkle, "Old Testament Prophecies Regarding the Nation of Israel," *The Southern Baptist Journal of Theology* 14.1 (Spring 2010), 19.

was to resolve the issue of Gentiles being included in the people of God, James sees the OT expectation of a restored Israel and Davidic Kingdom as being fulfilled presently![10] The restoration of Israel is happening through the growth of the Church. The story of the Church is the continuation of the story of the renewed Israel.

So Acts is all about the restoration of Israel.[11] Luke intentionally frames the whole narrative around the dawning of the kingdom (Acts 1:6 and 28:23). Christ sent His people to the Jews first, but they wanted nothing to do with their savior. Later in Acts, Paul describes his call to King Agrippa to preach to the Gentiles. Then he says "for this reason" the Jews tried to kill him (Acts 26:21). They forgot their reason for existence, and in fact, were opposed to it. So Luke closes his letter with Paul quoting Isaiah 6 about the hardness of their hearts and records Paul saying, "Therefore let it be known to you that this salvation of God has been sent to the Gentiles; they will listen" (Acts 28:28).

As we conclude our look at the Gospels and Acts, Chris Wright's words are a fitting transition: "The message therefore seems unanimous. Both Jesus himself and his immediate interpreters tell us that in the events of his arrival, life, death, resurrection and exaltation, God had acted decisively for the redemption and restoration of his people Israel in fulfillment of the whole range of OT prophecy that he would do so. To this they were called urgently to respond

---

10. Wright, "A Christian Approach to Old Testament Prophecy Concerning Israel," 16.
11. David L. Tiede, "The Exaltation of Jesus and the Restoration of Israel in Acts 1," *Harvard Theological Review* 79.1-3 (Jan/April/July, 1986), 278-86.

there and then as a present reality, not as some still future hope. 'The time is fulfilled...'."[12]

---

12. Wright, "A Christian Approach to Old Testament Prophecy Concerning Israel," 14-15.

# 8

# Galatians

It is probably no surprise that the writings of the Apostle Paul are crystal clear on the relationship of the Church and Israel. We start with Galatians due to its emphasis and clarity on this topic.[1] In many ways, the whole letter is about the relationship between Israel and the Church.[2] Some agitating false teachers came along and were teaching the Church that they needed to obey the Law to be true Israel, the real people of God.

Paul had been accused of being dependent on Jerusalem for his gospel and for distorting that gospel. These agitators wanted to correct him and "complete" the Galatian believers.

---

1. See Thomas R. Schreiner, *Galatians* (Grand Rapids: Zondervan, 2010), 57-58, 99, 130, 382, 394, as well as the commentary on the following verses; A. Blake White, *Galatians: A Theological Interpretation* (Frederick, MD: New Covenant Media, 2011) and Douglas J. Moo, *Galatians* (Grand Rapids: Baker Academic, 2013) on the relevant passages.
2. See my *The Abrahamic Promises in Galatians* (Frederick, MD: New Covenant Media, 2013).

So Paul begins by defending his message and his call. He starts autobiographical but quickly goes theological. Faith—and faith alone—is all that is necessary to be a part of the people of God.

## SONS OF ABRAHAM

Galatians 3:7 reads, "Know then that it is those of faith who are the sons of Abraham."[3] That is precisely the thesis of this book. Those of faith (the Church) are the sons of Abraham, that is, Israel. Those who believe in Jesus are the children of Abraham. I feel like writing that one more time since it's so clear, but I won't.

## THE SINGULAR OFFSPRING OF ABRAHAM

Galatians 3:16 is hugely important for the relationship between Israel and the Church. It reads, "Now the promises were made to Abraham and to his offspring. It does not say, 'And to offsprings,' referring to many, but referring to one, 'And to your offspring,' who is Christ." The God-breathed Word says that Jesus is *the* heir of the Abrahamic promise. He *alone* is the Jew who kept the covenant.[4] He is the *singular*

---

3. On the four-fold nature of Abraham's seed, see Reisinger, *Abraham's Four Seeds*; Gentry and Wellum, *Kingdom Through Covenant*, 115, 632-33, 696; Wellum, "Relationship Between the Covenants," 133-35.
4. LaRondelle, *The Israel of God in Prophecy*, 95. Russell Moore is worth quoting at length: For the new covenant apostles, Jew-Gentile unity is pivotal to the early church. It is about more than human relational harmony. Instead, it acknowledges that God's kingdom purposes are in Christ. He is the last man and the true Israel, the bearer of the Spirit. A Jewish person who clings to the tribal markings of the old covenant acts as though the eschaton has not arrived, as though one were still waiting for the promised seed. Both Jews and Gentiles must instead see their identities not in themselves or in the flesh but in Jesus Christ and in him alone.

offspring of Abraham. He embodies and sums up Israel. As the Messiah, what is true of Him is true of them. Paul says much the same in 2 Corinthians 1:20: "For all the promises of God find their Yes in him."

This was to be expected. Recall that in the section on Genesis, I wrote, "The plot of Genesis is preparing us to expect a singular offspring of the woman (and of Abraham) who will bring blessing to the nations." Jesus Himself said that Moses "wrote of me" (John 5:46). The whole Bible is about Jesus.[5] So, who is Israel? Jesus.

> Jesus is the descendant of Abraham, the one who deserves the throne of David. He is the obedient Israel who inherits the blessings of the Mosaic covenant. He is the propitiation of God's wrath. He is the firstborn from the dead, the resurrection and the life. Those who are in Christ – whether Jew or Gentile – receive with him all the eschatological blessings that are due to him. In him, they are all, whether Jew or Gentile, sons of God – not only in terms of relationship with the Father but also in terms of promised inheritance (Rom. 8:12-17). In Christ, they all – whether Jew or Gentile – are sons of Abraham, the true circumcision, the holy nation, and the household and commonwealth of God (Ga. 3:23-4:7; Eph 2-3; Col 2:6-15; 3:3-11; 1 Pet 2:9-10)... Both covenant theology and Dispensationalism, however, often discuss Israel and the church without taking into account the Christocentric nature of biblical eschatology. The future restoration of Israel has never been promised to the unfaithful, unregenerate members of the nation (John 3:3-10; Rom 2:25-29) – only to the faithful remnant. The church is not Israel, at least not in a direct, unmediated sense. The remnant of Israel – a biological descendant of Abraham, a circumcised Jewish firstborn son who is approved of by God for his obedience to the covenant – receives all of the promises due to him. Israel is Jesus of Nazareth, who, as promised to Israel, is raised from the dead and marked out with the Spirit (Ezek. 37:13-14; Rom 1:2-4). . . . Dispensationalists are right that only ethnic Jews receive the promised future restoration, but Paul makes clear that the "seed of Abraham" is singular, not plural (Gal. 3:16). Only the circumcised can inherit the promised future for Israel. All believers – Jew and Greek, slave and free, male and female – are forensically Jewish firstborn sons of God (Gal. 3:28). They are in Christ... In Christ, I inherit all the promises due to Abraham's offspring so that everything that is true of him is true of me... The future of Israel then does belong to Gentile believers but only because they are in union with a Jewish Messiah" "Personal and Cosmic Eschatology," in Theology for the Church, ed. Daniel L. Akin (Nashville: B&H Academic, 2007), 867-68, 906-07; idem., *The Kingdom of Christ*, 117-19.

5. Richard B. Hays writes, "Paul's understanding of Jesus Christ as the one true heir of the promise to Abraham is the essential theological presupposition for his

## SONS AND HEIRS OF ABRAHAM

Recall that the Messiah is a "corporate personality." He represents His people so that what is true of Him is true of His people.⁶ So because the offspring of Abraham is singular in the Messiah, it is plural in the people of that Messiah. Israel is reshaped around Israel's King. We see this just a few verses later in the same chapter:

> For in Christ Jesus you are all sons of God, through faith. For as many of you as were baptized into Christ have put on Christ. There is neither Jew nor Greek, there is neither slave nor free, there is no male and female, for you are all one in Christ Jesus. And if you are Christ's, then you are Abraham's offspring, heirs according to promise. (Gal. 3:26-29).

These verses are so clear but somehow overlooked in discussions of the Church and Israel. In Christ, *all* are sons of God. Whoever is in Christ is a son of God. "There is neither Jew nor Greek." There is no difference between Jew or Gentile in the new covenant. There is no distinction. In the new age, one should not distinguish Israel and the Church. Do not separate what God in Christ has joined. All

---

hermeneutical strategies," *Echoes of Scripture in the Letters of Paul* (London: Yale University Press, 1989), 121.

6. Richard B. Hays writes, "The way of salvation history runs through Jesus, and those who will not follow are in effect no longer part of the elect people. Thus the church becomes Israel, or, to put it more precisely, Israel after the resurrection of Jesus is composed entirely of those who believe and follow the prophet whom God has raised up," *The Moral Vision of the New Testament*, 419.

are one in the Messiah. "If you are Christ's, then you are Abraham's offspring, heirs according to promise." If you are in Christ, you are the offspring of Abraham.[7] As one has asked, "How could language state it any more conclusively and unambiguously?"[8] If you are part of the Church, you are Israel because you are united to Israel's Messiah. If you are in Christ, you are an heir of the promises made to Abraham. I appreciate the clarity of the NLT on this verse: "And now that you belong to Christ, you are the true children of Abraham. You are his heirs, and God's promise to Abraham belongs to you." Turns out, what many children sing is better theology than most realize: "Father Abraham had many sons, (and if in Christ), you are one of them and so am I!" So, who is Israel? Jesus, and the people of Jesus, namely, the Church.

## CHILDREN OF JERUSALEM ABOVE

In Galatians 4:21-31, we have the example of Hagar and Sarah. The central question is, "Who are the true children

---

7. Bruce W. Longenecker writes, "By means of their union with Christ (cf. 3.26-28), Christians are joined to the single seed of Abraham and thereby find themselves to be the collective 'descendants of Abraham.'" *The Triumph of Abraham's God: The Transformation of Identity in Galatians* (Nashville: Abingdon Press, 1998), 133; Similarly, France notes, "In Jesus himself the hopes and promises of Old Testament Israel are all coming to their fulfillment. He represents Israel as it should have been, and in him, and derivatively in his disciples, the true people of God is now located. Membership of God's people is no longer a matter of race. There is a place now for Gentiles alongside the minority of the Jewish nation who have responded to Jesus' teaching and become the nucleus of the Israel of the messianic age." "Old Testament Prophecy and the Future of Israel," 73; Gentry and Wellum, *Kingdom Through Covenant*, 106, 690.
8. LaRondelle, *The Israel of God in Prophecy*, 108. Yet Ryrie flabbergastingly states, "Believing Jews and believing Gentiles, which together make up the church in this age, continue to be distinguished in the New Testament." *Dispensationalism*, 148.

of Abraham?"[9] Perhaps the agitators had used this story to persuade the Galatian Christians to join them. Regardless, Paul interprets the story "allegorically" (Gal. 4:24), practicing a little "hermeneutical jujitsu."[10] Paul's argument was that Abraham had two sons, one (Ishmael) by Hagar and one (Isaac) by Sarah. The Jewish people are children of Hagar. They were born through human effort (*sarx*). They come from Mount Sinai and are children of the old covenant. Worst of all, they are slaves because their mother was a slave. Believers are children of Sarah. They are born through God's promise. They are part of the Jerusalem above, children of the new covenant. They are free because their mother was a free woman.

When Paul says that the Jerusalem above is our mother, he has Psalm 87 and the vision of glorious Zion in mind:

> Among those who know me I mention Rahab and Babylon behold, Philistia and Tyre, with Cush —"This one was born there," they say. And of Zion it shall be said, "This one and that one were born in her"; for the Most High himself will establish her. The LORD records as he registers the peoples, "This one was born there." (Ps. 87:4-6)

The Psalmist envisions a day when the Gentiles will be born in Jerusalem, the city of God. Though not biologically

---

9. See my *Galatians: A Theological Interpretation* (Frederick, MD: New Covenant Media, 2011), 119-34.
10. Hays, *Echoes of Scripture*, 112.

Jewish, Gentiles will be "registered" as such. The fulfillment of this Psalm was happening with the Galatian Christians, whose mother is the Jerusalem above.

Then Paul quotes from Isaiah's new exodus vision:

> Rejoice, O barren one who does not bear; break forth and cry aloud, you who are not in labor! For the children of the desolate one will be more than those of the one who has a husband. (Isa. 54:1 in Gal. 4:27)

Isaiah 54, which comes right after the vision of the suffering Servant (ch. 53), is about the new covenant, or to use his own language, the "covenant of peace" (Isa. 54:10). The old covenant people of God were barren and fruitless but it would not always be that way. They should "sing" because God would do a work to make them fruitful again. Yahweh says, "For a brief moment I deserted you, but with great compassion I will gather you" (Isa. 54:7). Sarah, the previously barren one and mother of Israel, will soon burst forth with offspring (Isa. 51:1-3).[11] Paul quotes this vision to say that the conversion of the Galatians to Christ is the fulfillment of Isaiah's vision. The abundance of children that Isaiah spoke of are believers in Gentile Churches.

Then Paul writes, "Now you, brothers, like Isaac are children of promise" (Gal. 4:28). Now you, Church, are Israel. You who trust in Christ are the heirs of the promises made to Israel. You are the true children of Abraham. Then

---

11. Hays, *Echoes of Scripture*, 118-21.

he concludes his allegory, saying, "So, brothers, we are not children of the slave but of the free woman" (Gal. 4:31). Regardless of ethnicity, if we are in Christ, Sarah is our mother.

## THE ISRAEL OF GOD

Paul closes Galatians with:

> Neither circumcision nor uncircumcision means anything; what counts is the new creation. Peace and mercy to all who follow this rule—to the Israel of God. (Gal. 6:15-16 NIV)

Lots of debate has surrounded the phrase "Israel of God."[12] Who is Paul referring to? Is he referring strictly to ethnic Jews or to the Church made up of Jews and Gentiles? This is an important passage for the thesis of this book. As you would expect by now, I think it is pretty clear that Paul is referring to the Church. Two main reasons lead me to this conclusion: the larger context and the immediate context.[13]

First, the larger context. The rule of exegesis is the same as that of real estate: location, location, location. On this question, the grammar and syntax are ambiguous, so as with every interpretive decision, context must be determinative.[14] We must examine the conclusion in light of the whole. And

---

12. See Robertson, *The Israel of God*, 38-46.
13. See Christopher W. Cowan, "Context is Everything: 'The Israel of God' in Galatians 6:16," *The Southern Baptist Journal of Theology* 14.3 (Fall 2010), 78-85.
14. I have used the NIV for this verse because I think it rightly takes *kai* as epexegetical.

as we have seen, in many ways, the point of the letter is that there is, in fact, no distinction between Jews and Gentiles.

Let me summarize again: anti-gospel agitators were trying to force the Gentiles to "Judaize" (*ioudaizein*), that is "to follow Jewish customs" (Gal. 2:14 NIV). They were saying that in order to become the true people of God, one must essentially become a Jew. Paul disagrees. Sharply. He is at pains to show that their teaching is emphatically false. It is anti-gospel. To force Gentiles to live like Jews is not walking in step with the truth of the gospel (Gal. 2:14). We've seen again and again that Gentiles become part of the children of God through faith in the Messiah. One becomes a child of Abraham, that is, a *Jew*, by being united to the Jewish King. I am not really sure how Paul could be any clearer on the matter. He's flogging a flat-lined pony here. To make a distinction between Jews and Gentiles stands at odds with the warp and woof of the whole letter.[15]

Second, the immediate context shows that the "Israel of God" includes Jews and Gentiles. Notice the structure of verses 15 and 16: in verse 15 Paul lays out the "rule" (*kanoni*) of the new creation, "neither circumcision nor uncircumcision means anything." In other words, ethnicity means nada. Paul uses this same "rule" in two other places: Galatians 5:6 and 1 Corinthians 7:19. "What counts is the new creation" (Gal. 6:15).

---

15. As Wright comments, "Those who insist on reading the Galatians passage as if it refers to an exclusively Jewish-Christian group should consider the way in which such an interpretation undoes at a stroke the entire argument of the rest of the letter," in "Jerusalem in the New Testament," 66n.22.

After laying out this "rule," Paul wishes peace and mercy on all who follow it, namely the Israel of God:

> Neither circumcision nor uncircumcision means anything; what counts is the new creation. Peace and mercy to all who follow this rule—to the Israel of God. (Gal. 6:15-16 NIV)

The Israel of God are those in Christ who agree with Paul that ethnicity means nothing in the new age. What is striking here is that the prayer for peace and mercy is excluded from those who would posit that ethnicity matters, that circumcision and uncircumcision matter, that there is a distinction between Jews and Gentiles in the economy of God.

Paul's mention of "peace" (*eirēnē*) and "mercy" (*eleos*), like we saw in Galatians 4:27, is from Isaiah's vision of a restored Israel: "For the mountains may depart and the hills be removed, but my steadfast love (*eleos*) shall not depart from you, and my covenant of peace (*eirēnēs*) shall not be removed, says the LORD, who has compassion (*hIleōs*) on you" (Isa. 54:10). He is wishing peace and mercy on the end-time restored people of God, namely Israel.[16]

In conclusion, if Paul is wishing peace and mercy on those

---

16. Beale writes, "Both gentile and Jewish believers are identified as the fulfillment of the Isa. 54 prophecy about 'peace and mercy' being on the one people of God, end-time Israel. The gentile Christians are part of this fulfillment of the restoration prophecy of Isa. 54. The *kai* signals a further explanation of the preceding 'them': the whole church is the inheritor of this prophecy as the true spiritual Israel." *A New Testament Biblical Theology*, 723.

who follow the rule of the new creation—the rule that says in essence what he already said: "There is neither Jew nor Gentile"—then he cannot be making a distinction between Jew and Gentile with the phrase "Israel of God" at the conclusion of this letter. This would not make sense in light of the immediate context or the larger context. In fact, it would undermine everything else he said about those who are in Christ by faith being Abraham's offspring and heirs according to promise. Therefore, based upon the larger and immediate context, "the Israel of God" in Galatians 6:16 includes any who are in Christ, Jew or Gentile.

# 9

# Romans

## NO ONE IS A JEW OUTWARDLY

Romans is also clear as crystal on the relationship between Israel and the Church. We begin early in the letter with Romans 2:28-29:

> For no one is a Jew who is merely one outwardly, nor is circumcision outward and physical. But a Jew is one inwardly, and circumcision is a matter of the heart, by the Spirit, not by the letter.

Here, the Holy Spirit through the Apostle Paul explicitly redefines what it means to be a Jew. In the new age that Jesus inaugurated, Jewishness no longer has to do with biology. This is the same thing Paul said above: circumcision matters not (Gal. 5:6, 6:15, 1 Cor. 7:19). Circumcision is no longer physical. In the new covenant era, being a Jew has to do with the heart. Now that Jesus has come, God is not concerned with circumcised foreskins but with circumcised hearts.

Of course, in saying this, the Apostle is standing on the shoulders of the prophets. Yet even earlier, Moses, at the end of his Deuteronomic sermon, lays out the blessings and curses of the covenant. He tells Israel that they will disobey and go into exile, but exile would not be the last word. One day, God would *exile* exile. He would gather His people, restore their fortunes, and "the Lord your God will circumcise your heart and the heart of your offspring, so that you will love the LORD your God with all your heart and with all your soul, that you may live" (Deut. 30:6). What interesting imagery! They have a heart problem. Something is keeping them from loving God as they should. The hearts of Israel are surrounded by foreskin that needs to be removed. Here is how Jeremiah put it:

> Circumcise yourselves to the LORD; remove the foreskin of your hearts, O men of Judah and inhabitants of Jerusalem; lest my wrath go forth like fire, and burn with none to quench it, because of the evil of your deeds."(Jer. 4:4, cf. Jer. 9:25-26, Deut. 10:16)

In speaking of the new age, Ezekiel picks up this imagery to speak of God coming to do heart surgery. He'll remove the "stony hearts" and replace them with a new heart and a new Spirit (Ezek. 36:25-27). God will change His people from the inside out, and they will obey Him from the heart. Jeremiah's new covenant prophecy of the Lord writing His law on the hearts of His people (Jer. 31:31-34) also pointed to this. Paul is telling the Romans that the new age is here and Jews are no longer Jews outwardly but inwardly (Rom. 2:29). Gentiles who trust Jesus and have Spirit-circumcised hearts are reckoned as Jews, regardless of ethnicity.[1]

## ABRAHAM, THE FATHER OF US ALL

In Romans 4, Paul shows that the blessing of forgiveness and righteousness was given to Abraham before he was circumcised, not after. The blessing of God is therefore not dependent on circumcision. This is *Hermeneutics 101* for Paul. Scripture is a sequential story. Genesis 15 precedes Genesis 17. The purpose for this sequence is, "To make [Abraham] the father of all who believe without being circumcised, so that righteousness would be counted to them as well, and to make him the father of the circumcised who are not merely circumcised but who also walk in the footsteps of the faith that our father Abraham had before he was circumcised" (Rom. 4:11-12). Then in verse 17, he quotes the promise of Genesis 17 that Abraham would be the father of many nations.[2] Gentiles are now included within the family and blessing of Abraham.

---

1. Wright writes, "Paul, in other words, is setting out a picture of the believing-in-the-Messiah people as the new reality to which ethnic Israel pointed forward but to which, outside the Messiah, they could not attain." *Justification*, 142-43.
2. See the above section on Genesis.

## THE LAND PROMISE

Almost in passing, Paul comments that Abraham and his offspring were promised to be "heir of the world" (Rom. 4:13). Paul knows the word for "land" (*gē*), but he says "world" (*kosmos*). He views the land promise in light of the whole story of Scripture. "Land" was significant long before Canaan. Eden was the first sacred space, so the land promise is built off the garden but points beyond itself like a signpost. Abraham himself knew this. Hebrews tells us that when he went to live in the promised land, "he was looking forward to the city that has foundations, whose designer and builder is God" (Heb. 11:10). To focus back on the signpost once you've arrived makes no sense. Once you get to Capitol Hill, don't return to gaze at the sign that reads, "Washington D.C.: 25 Miles." As we saw in Galatians 4, Jerusalem on earth pointed forward to the Jerusalem above, who is our mother. Or as Hebrews puts it, "You have come to Mount Zion and to the city of the living God, the heavenly Jerusalem" (Heb. 12:22).

In the current era of salvation history, being in Christ has replaced being in the land, but there is more to come. The land finds its ultimate fulfillment in the new earth. Paul says that Abraham and his international offspring are "heirs" (*klēronomon,* Romans 4:13). Significantly, he only uses this word one other time in Romans. It comes in the section where he writes of the whole creation being set free from its bondage to corruption (Rom. 8:17-22).[3] To focus on a slim piece of real estate east of the Mediterranean is just too small.

Jesus has more in store, something global: a whole renovated earth.[4] And whoever is in Christ is a "co-heir." Jesus inherits all of God's promises, and so do believers by sharing in what He has received.

## NO LONGER "NOT MY PEOPLE"

In Romans 9:24-26, Paul writes,

> Even us whom he has called, not from the Jews only but also from the Gentiles? As indeed he says in Hosea, "Those who were not my people I will call 'my people,' and her who was not beloved I will call 'beloved.'" "And in the very place where it was said to them, 'You are not my people,' there they will be called 'sons of the living God.'"

Paul combines Hosea 2:23 with 1:10 to substantiate the fact that God is calling not only Jews, but also Gentiles.

In Hosea 1, the Lord had told Hosea to marry a whore because Israel is acting like a whore in her forsaking of the Lord. She gives birth to three children, the second and third of which are named, *No Mercy* and *Not My People,* for Israel is

---

3. Beale, *A New Testament Biblical Theology*, 761-62.
4. See my *The Abrahamic Promises in Galatians*, 37-44; Oren Martin, *Bound for the Promise Land: The Land Promise in God's Redemptive Plan* (Downers Grove, IL: InterVarsity Press, 2015); Robertson, *The Israel of God*, 3-31; Gary M. Burge, *Jesus and the Land: The New Testament Challenge to 'Holy Land' Theology* (Grand Rapids: Baker Academic, 2010); O. Palmer Robertson, *Understanding the Land of the Bible: A Biblical-Theological Guide* (Phillipsburg, NJ: P&R, 1996); Beale, *A New Testament Biblical Theology*, 750-72; Dalrymple, *These Brothers of Mine*, 63-78.

"not my people, and I am not your God" (Hos. 1:9). But there is hope: "Yet the number of the children of Israel shall be like the sand of the sea, which cannot be measured or numbered. And in the place where it was said to them, 'You are not my people,' it shall be said to them, 'Children of the living God'" (Hos. 1:9-10). Judgment is coming on unfaithful Israel, but judgment is not the final word.

The references to sand of the sea and numerous offspring obviously point back to the promise God made to Abraham: "I will surely bless you, and I will surely multiply your offspring as the stars of heaven and as the sand that is on the seashore" (Gen. 22:17). Hosea refers that promise to the children of Israel; Paul refers it to the calling of both Jews and Gentiles. The restoration of Israel is happening through the growth of the Church.[5] In other words, believing Gentiles are "children of the living God" and included within Israel because of what Christ has done.

Hosea 2 also speaks words of judgment against Israel (Hos. 2:1-13), followed by words of hope (Hos. 2:14-23): the Lord promises to remove idolatry from their midst, to make a covenant with them, to be their husband once again, and to make them know the Lord. In that day, He will have mercy on *No Mercy* and will say to *Not My People*, "You are My people." Hosea is speaking of the restoration of Israel, but Paul quotes him to refer to the inclusion of Gentiles in the people of God.[6]

---

5. Storms writes, "The calling of Gentiles from among every tribe, tongue, people, and nation is the prophesied restoration of Israel, for the church is the continuation and maturation of Israel's believing remnant." *Kingdom Come*, 200.

# BEAUTIFUL FEET ANNOUNCING THE END OF EXILE

Romans 10:14-17 is a famous "missionary passage." Rightly so:

> How then will they call on him in whom they have not believed? And how are they to believe in him of whom they have never heard? And how are they to hear without someone preaching? And how are they to preach unless they are sent? As it is written, "How beautiful are the feet of those who preach the good news!" But not all the Israelites accepted the good news. For Isaiah says, "Lord, who has believed our message?" (Rom. 10:14-16)

What is often left out is the OT quotation. In speaking of the need for gospel promoters, Paul quotes from Isaiah's new exodus prophecy. The reference to the beautiful feet bringing good news comes from Isaiah 52:7, which is about the good news of the redemption of Israel. Romans 10:16 is from Isaiah 53:1, which, of course, leads to the Servant who

---

6. Douglas J. Moo writes, "Therefore we must conclude that this text reflects a hermeneutical supposition for which we find evidence elsewhere in Paul and in the NT: that OT predictions of a renewed Israel find their fulfillment in the church." *The Epistle to the Romans* (Grand Rapids: Eerdmans, 1996), 613. So also Thomas R. Schreiner: "Paul conceives of Hosea's prophecy as fulfilled in the calling of the Gentiles. The church is the renewed Israel and the arena in which God's promises find their fulfillment." *Romans* (Grand Rapids: Baker Academic, 1998), 528.

suffers on Israel's behalf.[7] Paul sees his own ministry to Jews and Gentiles as a partial fulfillment of the end of Israel's exile.

## ALL ISRAEL WILL BE SAVED

Romans 11 is often misread, assumed, and thrown about as if it closes the conversation on the Church/Israel topic. I can't count how many times I have been told, "But Romans 11 teaches the future restoration of ethnic Israel," full stop, as if that undemonstrated assertion is all there is to say.

Now, it is a dense chapter, and many solid exegetes disagree on how to interpret it. And I do not claim to have *the* new covenant view, but I hope to show the reading that best fits the hermeneutic that has been shown throughout.[8]

One main question is driving Paul in Romans chapter 11: *Has God completely rejected Israel?* That's how he starts: "I ask, then, has God rejected his people" (Rom. 11:1)? To feel the force of it, we could paraphrase it as, "Has God *completely* rejected the Jews?" Lest his readers lose track, he repeats himself in verse 11: "So I ask, did they stumble in order that they might fall?" Again, we could read it as, "That they might *totally* fall?" His answer to the question in both instances is the same: no way.

But the question is a legitimate one that doubtless many in that day were asking. Paul himself says in the previous verse that all day long God had held out His hands "to a disobedient

---

7. Later, in Romans 15:21, Paul quotes again from Isaiah (52:15).
8. Solid theologians who have a similar hermeneutic as this book, but who hold a "futuristic" view of this chapter include Tom Schreiner, Doug Moo, John Piper, and Jason Meyer, to name a few.

and contrary people" (Rom. 10:21). In 1 Thessalonians 2:16, we read that God's wrath has come on the Jews forever (*eis telos*). Jesus had told the Jews, "The Kingdom of God will be taken away from you and given to a people producing its fruit" (Matt. 21:43). In His rebuke of the Jewish leaders, Jesus said, "Fill up, then, the measure of your fathers" (Matt. 23:32, cf. Gen. 15:16) and "on you may come all the righteous blood shed on earth, from the blood of righteous Abel to the blood of Zechariah the son of Barachiah, whom you murdered between the sanctuary and the altar" (Matt. 23:35). Jesus pleaded with the Jews: "O Jerusalem, Jerusalem, the city that kills the prophets and stones those who are sent to it! How often would I have gathered your children together as a hen gathers her brood under her wings, and you were not willing" (Matt. 23:37).

The pagan Pilate (and his lady-friend) were hesitant to crucify Jesus and gave the Jews a chance to change their mind. Pilate would release Jesus and crucify Barabbas if they agreed. But the leaders told the Jewish people to "destroy Jesus" (Matt. 27:20). They "all" said, "Let him be crucified" (Matt. 27:22)! Pilate again hesitates, but they shout, "All the more, 'Let him be crucified'" (Matt. 27:23)! Pilate literally washes his hands and says this is on them and not him. Astonishingly, "All the people (*pas ho laos*) answered, 'His blood be on us and on our children'" (Matt. 27:25)!

John records the Jews threatening Pilate, saying, "If you don't put him to death, you are no friend of Caesar." Pilate asks them, "Shall I crucify your king?" Astoundingly, they reply, "We have no king but Caesar" (John 19:15). The Jewish people calling Caesar their only king? Bone-chilling.

After the Jews reviled Paul and his message, he said, "Your blood be on your own heads" (Acts 18:6). Luke closed his second volume with Paul telling the Jews that their hearts were dull and now "This salvation of God has been sent to the Gentiles; they will listen" (Acts 28:28).

So asking whether or not God is *totally* done with the Jews is a legitimate question. In Romans 11, Paul shows how salvation is still available to any Jew who trusts in Christ. Anyone who trusts in Christ can and will be saved, including Jews.

Another overlooked fact is the abundance of time indicators in the chapter. Interpreters often assume that Romans 11 is about the future, but Paul repeatedly makes it clear that his concern is a present one. Paul's focus is on the $1^{st}$ century, not the $21^{st}$ century:

- "Has God rejected his people? By no means! For I myself am an Israelite" (Rom. 11:1). (Paul in the first century is current proof that God has not totally rejected Israel since he himself is a Jewish recipient of the Messiah's blessing.)

- "So too at the *present* time there is a remnant" (Rom. 11:5, emphasis mine).

- "*Now* I am speaking to you Gentiles" (Rom. 11:13, emphasis mine).

- "I magnify *my* ministry" (Rom. 11:13, emphasis mine). (He is focused on his ministry in the first century.)

- "For just as you were at one time disobedient to God but *now* have received mercy because of their disobedience" (Rom. 11:30). ("Now" in the first century.)

- "So they have *now* been disobedient" (Rom. 11:31, emphasis mine).

- "By the mercy shown to you they also may *now* receive mercy" (Rom. 11:31).

So it is clear that this chapter is not about the future, but Paul's present.

In Romans 9-11, Paul explains that Israel's rejection of their Messiah is not failure on God's part. He never promised to save every Israelite, but only the elect. There is an Israel within Israel. "Not all who are descended from Israel belong to Israel" (Rom. 9:6). There are children of promise and children of the flesh *within* the physical offspring of Abraham (Rom. 9:6-13). God has not "rejected his people whom he foreknew" (Rom. 11:2). Part of Israel has been hardened, but not all. "What then? Israel failed to obtain what it was seeking. The elect obtained it, but the rest were hardened" (Rom. 11:7).

The point of Romans 11 is that Israel's fall is not total. No, through their trespass, salvation has come to the Gentiles to make Israel jealous, and "some" of them will be saved (Rom. 11:14). *Some* ethnic Jews, not all. Lest the Gentiles become arrogant about this new situation, he warns them. In doing so, he says that Gentiles are wild olive shoots grafted in, now sharing in the nourishing root of the olive tree. This word for "share" (*sygkoinōnos*) is similar in form to the words Paul uses of the same reality in Ephesians 3:6: "The Gentiles are fellow heirs (*sygklēronoma*), members of the same body (*syssōma*), and partakers (*symmetocha*) of the promise in Christ Jesus through the gospel." Each of these words begins with *syn*, which means "together with." The Gentiles are together with Israel in the root, in the inheritance, in the body, and in the promise. In other words, like the prophets prophesied, Gentiles have been grafted *into* Israel.

Now we come to the controversial passage. Romans 11:25-27 reads,

> Lest you be wise in your own sight, I do not want you to be unaware of this mystery, brothers: a partial hardening has come upon Israel, until the fullness of the Gentiles has come in. And in this way all Israel will be saved, as it is written, "The Deliverer will come from Zion, he will banish ungodliness from Jacob;" "and this will be my covenant with them when I take away their sins."

Paul doesn't want his audience to miss this. A partial hardening has come upon Israel. Many interpreters wrongly read this hardening in temporal rather than quantitative terms. It literally reads, "a hardening from part in Israel" (*pōrōsis apo merous tǭ Israēl*). Part of Israel has been hardened "until (*arxi*) the fullness of the Gentiles has come in."[9] With "until," Paul is saying this will be the state of things throughout this present era. He uses the same word with regard to the Lord's Meal, when he says we proclaim the Lord's death "until" he comes (1 Cor. 11:26). Or later he says that Jesus must reign "until" he has put all his enemies under his feet (1 Cor. 15:25). So this hardening of a portion of Israel will endure during this whole present era until its goal is reached at the end of history.[10]

The fullness of the Gentiles refers to the full number of elect Gentiles in history.[11] At this stage in salvation history, most Jews have been hardened, but not all. The elect obtained it, but the rest were hardened (Rom. 11:7). "Some" will be saved as Gentiles are being saved (Rom. 11:14). "And in this way all Israel will be saved." Again, interpreters often take "in this way" as temporal. So they read it as, "Gentiles will be

---

9. 2 Corinthians 3:14-16 says, "But their minds were hardened. For to this day, when they read the old covenant, that same veil remains unlifted, because only through Christ is it taken away. Yes, to this day whenever Moses is read a veil lies over their hearts. But when one turns to the Lord, the veil is removed."
10. O. Palmer Robertson, "Is There a Distinctive Future for Ethnic Israel in Romans 11?" in *Perspectives on Evangelical Theology* ed. Kenneth S. Kantzer and Stanley N. Gundry (Grand Rapids: Baker, 1979), 219-20; idem., *The Israel of God*, 179-81.
11. In personal correspondence, Douglas Goodin suggests that "the fullness of the Gentiles" may refer to the time of the destruction of the Jerusalem temple in AD70. He bases his view on the similarity of language used by Paul and Luke. Romans 11:25 reads, "until the fullness of the Gentiles has come in" (*arxi hou to plērōma tōn ethnōn eiselthę̄*) and Luke 21:24, referring to the destruction of Jerusalem, reads "until the times of the Gentiles are fulfilled" (*achri hou plērōthōsin kairoi ethnōn*). So the hardening in his view is temporal. There was a judicial hardening of Israel until God's full judgment was poured out on Jerusalem through Rome, after that the hardening was removed and salvation is now freely available to all Jews who trust in Christ. This particular reading of Rom. 11:25 would fit my overall reading of the whole section.

saved *then* all Israel will be saved." But that is not what the word *houtōs* means, here or elsewhere. The ESV nails it here; it is modal, not temporal. *In this way* all Israel will be saved. Paul is explaining the *manner in which* all Israel will be saved. God has hardened part of Israel, is saving Gentiles, which is causing some Jews to become jealous and so be saved—and *in this way*, all Israel will be saved. We will unpack just who "all Israel" is below.

Then Paul provides important OT grounding:

> As it is written, "The Deliverer will come from Zion, he will banish ungodliness from Jacob"; "and this will be my covenant with them when I take away their sins."

Here, Paul is combining several OT promises. Getting these verses right is crucial because 11:26b explains 11:26a. In other words, we learn what "all Israel will be saved" means from learning what these OT promises mean. The main passage Paul is drawing on should not surprise us at this point: Isaiah 59, where God promises to rescue His people, reign as King, and dwell with His people. Right after the verse Paul quotes, the LORD speaks of this future covenant where God will do the inward work that Jeremiah and Ezekiel spoke of as well (Isa. 59:21). So Isaiah 59 is a "new covenant" promise. This is what Jesus came to accomplish *in His first coming.*

Interestingly, Isaiah 59:20 says, "A Redeemer will come *to* Zion." Paul says, the Redeemer "will come *from* Zion (*ek Zion*)." Did Paul just slip? No, the Spirit is moving him along. With "from Zion," Paul is making a couple of points. First, he is quoting a passage that is future from Isaiah's perspective but past from his own perspective. The Messiah came from Zion. He is Israel's Messiah for the world. Second, with "from Zion," Paul is alluding to two other prophecies. Psalm 14:7 speaks of the future restoration of Israel. It reads, "Oh, that salvation for Israel would come out of Zion (*ek Zion*)! When the LORD restores the fortunes of his people, let Jacob rejoice, let Israel be glad." The other prophecy is from Isaiah's earlier vision where he describes, in poetic form, what the world will look like when God restores Israel. Isaiah 2 is a vision of the latter days where the Lord's mountain will be the highest, the nations will flow to it, "for out of Zion (*ek gar Zion*) shall go the law" (Isa. 2:2-3, cf. Micah 4:2). Rather than seeking the instruction of the Lord (Torah) coming from Zion, the Apostle sees the fulfillment in the King coming from Zion since Christ is the "culmination of the law" (Rom. 10:4 NIV).

Another passage Paul includes in Romans 11:26-27 is Isaiah 27:9.[12] Isaiah 27 is about the deliverance of Israel. God promises that "in days to come Jacob shall take root, Israel shall blossom and put forth shoots and fill the whole world with fruit" and "the guilt of Jacob will be atoned for" and the fruit of this atonement will be the removal of idols (Isa. 27:6, 9). He then speaks of Gentiles being included within Israel: "those who were lost in the land of Assyria and those who

---

12. The quote is clearer in Greek. The LXX of Isaiah 27:9 reads "*hotan aphelōmai autou tēn hamartian.*" Romans 11:27 reads "*hotan aphelōmai tas hamartias autōn.*"

were driven out to the land of Egypt will come and worship the LORD on the holy mountain at Jerusalem" (Isa. 27:13).

The last passage alluded to here in Romans 11:26 is Jeremiah 31 and the promise of the new covenant. When any Jew heard language of "taking away sin" and "covenant" they would immediately think of Jeremiah's grand promise:

> Behold, the days are coming, declares the LORD, when I will make a new covenant with the house of Israel and the house of Judah, not like the covenant that I made with their fathers on the day when I took them by the hand to bring them out of the land of Egypt, my covenant that they broke, though I was their husband, declares the LORD. For this is the covenant that I will make with the house of Israel after those days, declares the LORD: I will put my law within them, and I will write it on their hearts. And I will be their God, and they shall be my people. And no longer shall each one teach his neighbor and each his brother, saying, 'Know the LORD,' for they shall all know me, from the least of them to the greatest, declares the LORD. For I will forgive their iniquity, and I will remember their sin no more. (Jeremiah 31:31–34)

Again, this passage finds fulfillment in the first coming of Jesus. This is what the Church celebrates every time we celebrate the Lord's Supper. The Deliverer has come and forgiven our sins. Many interpreters assume these verses are about the future, but it should be clear from the OT background that the coming Redeemer refers not to the second coming, but to the first coming of Jesus. These are new covenant passages and the new covenant was inaugurated with His first coming.[13] They are also all passages that speak of the inclusion of Gentiles within the people of God.

Now we are at a place to answer the question, *What does Paul mean by, "all Israel"?* Before answering, it is important to state what is emphatically not in this chapter: a rebuilt temple, anything about the land, a reconstitution of geopolitical Israel, a millennial kingdom for ethnic Israel, etc.[14] These sorts of things are often assumed to be included, but they are simply not found in this chapter. Contrary to many (especially American) interpreters, Romans 11 is not about a future millennium for the nation of Israel.

Context makes it clear that there are three legitimate options for who "all Israel" is. Many interpreters take the view that all Israel refers to "all" ethnic Jews who will trust in Christ at the last day when Christ returns.[15] It is important to note that these interpreters do not separate the Church

---

13. David G. Peterson, *Transformed by God: New Covenant Life and Ministry* (Downers Grove: IVP Academic, 2012), 130-32.
14. For example, in his commentary on these verses, John MacArthur says that all Israel are "all the elect Jewish people alive at the end of the Tribulation… the Lord Jesus Christ's millennial rule will be associated with Mt. Zion." One wonders where he gets the "Tribulation" or the "Millennium" in this passage. Neither is anywhere to be found anywhere in Romans 9-11, or all of Romans for that matter. *The MacArthur Study Bible* (Nashville: Nelson, 1997), 1715.
15. Moo, *The Epistle to the Romans*, 710-29; Schreiner, *Romans*, 611-623; Jason C. Meyer, *The End of the Law: Mosaic Covenant in Pauline Theology* (Nashville: B&H Academic, 2009), 177-229; Piper D. Martyn Lloyd-Jones, *The Church and the Last Things* (Wheaton: Crossway, 1998), 113.; Kim Riddlerbarger, *Amillennialism: Understanding the End Times* (Grand Rapids: Baker, 2003), 180-94.

and Israel. They view these Jews as those who will join the Church at the second coming and so be saved in a future mass conversion. Most don't think "all" means "all" here.[16] But "many" Jews will be saved at this last minute altar call given by the Lord Jesus Himself.[17]

Others would agree with my view of the "present" concern of the chapter, and define "all Israel" as all elect Jews who will come to Christ throughout history.[18] They would agree with much of what I have articulated, but would say the immediate context lends toward viewing "all Israel" as only ethnic Jews. A good case can be made for this view.

I take "all Israel" as referring to anyone—Jew or Gentile—who trusts in Christ. In other words, it is all the elect. In yet other words, all Israel is the Church. Though both of these last options are viable, five reasons cause me to believe that Paul is referring to the Church with "all Israel" in Romans 11:26.[19]

---

16. But as Robertson puts it, "In this context, 'all' can hardly mean 'most.'" *Israel of God*, 183.
17. Besides the exegetical difficulty, this brings evangelistic difficulty as well. The view could hinder gospel urgency among Jewish people. It would also seem logical to urge those who reject Christ to consider Judaism since if Jesus returns in our day, presumably they'd be part of the "all" Israel who will get saved at the *parousia*.
18. Ben L. Merkle, "Romans 11 and the Future of Ethnic Israel," *JETS* 43.4 (December), 709-21; Charles M. Horne, "The Meaning of the Phrase 'And Thus All Israel Will Be Saved'," *JETS* 21.4 (December 1978), 329-34; Storms, *Kingdom Come*, 303-34. Robertson, "*Is There a Distinctive Future for Ethnic Israel in Romans 11?*," 209-227. Note that Robertson later changed his view.
19. See Augustine, Luther, Calvin, Barth, Hays, *Moral Vision* 416-17; Wright, "Jerusalem in the New Testament," 65-67; idem., *The Climax of the Covenant* (Minneapolis: Fortress Press, 1993), 231-57; idem., *Paul and the Faithfulness of God, Book Two* (Minneapolis: Fortress Press, 2013), 1156-1259; Robertson, *The Israel of God*, 167-92; Paul Williamson, "Covenant," in *New Dictionary of Biblical Theology*, 428.

First, there is the immediate context. He has just finished saying that Gentiles are grafted *into* Israel. This is what we saw again and again in the prophets. The olive shoots are grafted into the olive tree (Rom. 11:17). When Paul says that part of Israel has been hardened "until the fullness of the Gentiles has come in" (Rom. 11:25), he means "until all elect Gentiles come into Israel." In chapter 10, Paul wrote that *everyone* who believes in Jesus will not be put to shame "for there is no distinction between Jew and Greek" (Rom. 10:11-12). He just said there is *no distinction* between Jews and Gentiles in Christ, which is exactly what I am saying Romans 11:26 says. Paul uses very similar language in Romans 10:13 as he does in Romans 11:26. In the former, he writes that *everyone* who calls on the name of the Lord *will be saved* (*sōthēsetai*). In the latter, he says that all Israel *will be saved* (*sōthēsetai*). "All Israel" consists of everyone who calls on the name of the Lord. They will be saved. Romans 10:18-21 quotes the OT a few times to speak of the end of the world, the nations and Israel's jealousy, and the Lord being found by the nations. He closes that section saying, "But of Israel he says, 'All day long I have held out my hands to a disobedient and contrary people" (Rom. 10:21).

Second is the larger context of Romans. Paul has already redefined Jewishness at the beginning of the letter. Readers of chapter 11 must not forget the earlier chapters. A Jew is no longer one outwardly, but inwardly (Rom. 2:28-29). Romans 4 spoke of Abraham as the father of both Jews and Gentiles. Romans 9 quoted Hosea to refer to the inclusion of Gentiles in Israel. So by the time we get to Romans 11, new covenant Israel has already been defined as including Gentiles.

Third, we have the even larger context of Pauline theology. We have only looked at Galatians so far, but we will see much the same below. All over the place, Paul defines Israel around the Messiah. If you are of Christ, then you are the children of Abraham (Gal. 3:29). He concludes his letter to the Galatians by calling Jews and Gentiles "the Israel of God" (Gal. 6:16).[20] We will demonstrate this with other texts in the next chapter.

Fourth is the meaning of "mystery" in Paul's letters. In Romans 11:25, Paul writes that he does not want the Romans to be unaware of "this mystery." The mystery is that part of Israel is hardened, which leads to the salvation of Gentiles, and in turn some Jews will be saved, and in this way all Israel will be saved (see Acts 13:46, 18:6). "Mystery" in Paul's writings does not refer to something hard to understand, but to revelation. It is something that was previously hidden, but is now revealed. He uses the word again at the close of this letter:

> Now to him who is able to strengthen you according to my gospel and the preaching of Jesus Christ, according to the revelation of the mystery that was kept secret for long ages but has now been disclosed and through the prophetic writings has been made known

---

20. Hays writes, "The 'Israel' of Romans 11:26 is the same as the 'Israel of God' in Galatians 6:16, a description of the elect eschatological people of God consisting of Jews and Gentiles together in Christ," *Moral Vision*, 417.

to all nations, according to the command of the eternal God, to bring about the obedience of faith— to the only wise God be glory forevermore through Jesus Christ! Amen.
(Rom 16:25–27)

The mystery was kept secret, but it is now disclosed to all nations. The command was to bring about the "obedience of faith." Paul sandwiches this letter with this apostolic goal. Romans 1:5 says that he was given his commission to "bring about the obedience of faith for the sake of his name among all the nations."

Paul uses this same word in the same way in Ephesians to speak of the inclusion of Gentiles within the Israel of God: "This mystery is that the Gentiles are fellow heirs, members of the same body, and partakers of the promise in Christ Jesus through the gospel"(Eph. 3:6). We'll unpack the specifics of this verse later, but here the mystery is Gentiles becoming fellow heirs with Israel and members of the same body. Paul's theology of the people of God in Romans is consistent with his theology of the people of God in the rest of his letters.

Fifth, we have the OT grounding.[21] We saw that Paul explains *all Israel being saved* by quoting passages about the first coming of Jesus to establish the new covenant, which includes Jews and Gentiles. In Paul's theology, the removal of sin from the people of God occurs at the cross and

---

21. Christopher R. Bruno, "The Deliverer From Zion: The Source(s) and Function of Paul's Citation in Romans 11:26-27," *Tyndale Bulletin* 59.1 (2008), 119-34.

resurrection, not at the second coming. As he put it a few chapters earlier, there is therefore *now* no condemnation for those in Christ (Rom. 8:1).

So Paul answers his own question by saying that God has not abandoned His people. Rather, He always only promised to save the elect, and in the new age He has expanded *Israel* to include Gentiles.

How should one conclude such a section? One cannot improve on the way the Spirit moved Paul to do so: "Oh, the depth of the riches and wisdom and knowledge of God! How unsearchable are his judgments and how inscrutable his ways" (Rom. 11:33)!

## THAT THE GENTILES MIGHT GLORIFY GOD

Our final passage in Romans is Romans 15:8-12:

> For I tell you that Christ became a servant to the circumcised to show God's truthfulness, in order to confirm the promises given to the patriarchs, and in order that the Gentiles might glorify God for his mercy. As it is written, "Therefore I will praise you among the Gentiles, and sing to your name." And again it is said, "Rejoice, O Gentiles, with his people." And again, "Praise the Lord, all you Gentiles, and let all the peoples extol him." And again Isaiah says, "The root of Jesse will come, even he who arises to rule the Gentiles; in him will the Gentiles hope." (Rom 15:8–12)

Right after encouraging Jewish and Gentile Christians to "welcome one another" (Rom. 15:7), Paul grounds his exhortation in the fact that Jesus became a servant to the circumcised to show God's faithfulness to His promises given to the patriarchs. (Many Dispensational interpreters think that God has not yet been faithful to these promises. Let's stick with Paul.) Then he says the purpose of God keeping those promises was "in order that the Gentiles might glorify God for his mercy" (Rom. 15:9). Then Paul quotes from the historical books, the Law, the poetic section, and the prophetic section of the OT to prove this point. Romans is clear that in the new age, Israel has been broadened to include all who trust in Christ, regardless of ethnicity.

# 10

# More Paul

We now turn to the key passages in the rest of Paul's letters where we will continue to see that the story of the Church is the continuation of the story of Israel because of Christ and the Spirit.

## OUR FATHERS AND ISRAEL ACCORDING TO THE FLESH

When Paul warns against idolatry in 1 Corinthians 10, he draws on the people of Israel as a negative example. That is not surprising. What is surprising is how he relates his Gentile audience to the Jews, when he writes, "I do not want you to be unaware, brothers, that our fathers were all under the cloud, and all passed through the sea" (1 Cor. 10:1). He calls the ancient people of Israel the fathers of the Corinthians![1]

---

1. Hays writes, "It may seem odd that Paul would describe the Israelites in the way in a letter addressed to the predominantly Gentile congregation at Corinth, who

That is because the Church is the continuation, fulfillment, and expansion of Israel. The Gentile Corinthians are children of Israel.[2] Israel's history is now the Church's history. The Gentile converts have been scripted into the one plan of God to rescue the world through the offspring of Abraham.

He concludes the exhortation by encouraging this Gentile church to "consider Israel according to the flesh" (1 Cor. 10:18).[3] After calling the Israelites the fathers of the Corinthian Christians, it is clear he sees them as the people of God. Paul often contrasts Spirit and flesh, so we are safe to conclude that old covenant unfaithful Israel is Israel according to the flesh and the faithful Church is Israel according to the Spirit.[4] Interestingly, when describing the idolatrous past of the Corinthians, he writes, "You know that when you were Gentiles, you were led astray to mute idols" (1 Cor. 12:2).[5] This is the same move he made back in 1 Corinthians 5 when he rebuked the Corinthians for putting up with sexual sin that is not even tolerated among the Gentiles (*ethnesin* – 1 Cor. 5:1). There is a sense in which these Gentile Christians are no longer Gentiles.

---

of course are not the physical descendants of Israel, but Paul's language reveals something essential about his understanding of the Church. His Gentile converts, he believes, have been grafted into the covenant people (cf. Rom. 11:17-24) in such a way that they belong to Israel (cf. Gal. 6:16). Thus, the story of Israel is for the Gentile Corinthians not somebody else's story; it is the story of their own authentic spiritual ancestors" *First Corinthians* (Louisville: John Knox Press, 1997), 160.

2. Hays, *Echoes of Scripture*, 95-97.
3. Here I am going with the ESV's footnote translation. I am not sure why they do not include *kata sarka* in their translation.
4. Gordon D. Fee, *The First Epistle to the Corinthians* (Grand Rapids: Eerdmans, 1987), 470 n. 38.
5. My translation. The ESV reads, "when you were pagans," but the word is *ethnē*, which is better translated as Gentiles.

## JESUS FULFILLS ALL THE PROMISES OF GOD

While not explicitly about the Church and Israel, I cannot pass over 2 Corinthians 1:20: "For all the promises of God find their Yes in him." All of God's promises are fulfilled in Jesus. All of them. Including, especially, and primarily the promises given to Israel. Jesus is the sole inheritor who then shares His riches with all of His children.

## THE NEW COVENANT

In 2 Corinthians 3, Paul shows that while the old covenant was glorious, the new is much more so. The Corinthians are a letter from Christ, written not on tablets of stone, but on tablets of human hearts. This is of course the language of Ezekiel's prophecy where God would come to Israel and replace their stony hearts with fleshly hearts so they could obey him fully (Ezek. 36:25-27). The Gentile Corinthians are beneficiaries of these promises.

And as we have seen, the language of "new covenant" is from Jeremiah's famous prophecy. Jeremiah said it was for "the house of Israel and the house of Judah." Paul applies it to the Church. It will not do to make up another new covenant. There is only one, and the Church is the recipient of its blessings. The people of God have been expanded to include Jews and Gentiles due to the work of Christ and the Spirit in the new age.

## THE NEW TEMPLE

In 2 Corinthians 6, Paul exhorts the Gentile church to avoid being unequally yoked with unbelievers. He gives the command, supports it with rhetorical questions and OT background, then restates the command. Here we go:

> Do not be unequally yoked with unbelievers. For what partnership has righteousness with lawlessness? Or what fellowship has light with darkness? What accord has Christ with Belial? Or what portion does a believer share with an unbeliever? What agreement has the temple of God with idols? For we are the temple of the living God; as God said, "I will make my dwelling among them and walk among them, and I will be their God, and they shall be my people. Therefore go out from their midst, and be separate from them, says the Lord, and touch no unclean thing; then I will welcome you, and I will be a father to you, and you shall be sons and daughters to me, says the Lord Almighty." Since we have these promises, beloved, let us cleanse ourselves from every defilement of body and spirit, bringing holiness to completion in the fear of God. (2 Cor. 6:14–7:1)

Paul asserts that the Corinthian believers are the temples of the living God (2 Cor. 6:16, cf. 1 Cor. 3:16-17, 6:19-20). He used similar language a few chapters earlier when speaking of the new covenant: "the Spirit of the living God" (2 Cor. 3:3).[6]

---

6. Scott J. Hafemann, *Second Corinthians* (Grand Rapids: Zondervan, 2000), 282. His whole exposition of this passage (277-89) is right on.

The fact that the Corinthians are indwelt by the Spirit makes them the temple.[7]

Then he grounds his assertion by quoting six OT passages: Leviticus 26:11-12, Ezekiel 37:27, Isaiah 52:11, Ezekiel 20:34, 2 Samuel 7:14, and Isaiah 43:6.[8] These contexts should be getting familiar by now. The Leviticus passage is a promise that God will dwell in the midst of His people Israel. It says, "I will make my dwelling among you" (Lev. 26:11), but Paul writes that God will dwell among "them" not "you," a subtle but important difference. Paul conflates a promise about the old covenant with a promise of the new covenant. After prophesying that God would give Israel new hearts and resurrection life, Ezekiel prophesies that God will make a covenant of peace with Israel and will dwell among "them" (Ezek. 37:27). He goes on to speak of gathering Israel under his servant David (Ezek. 37:24-28). These promises are finding their fulfillment in the Spirit-filled Corinthian community. Scott Hafemann writes, "By interpreting Leviticus 26:11-12 in terms of Ezekiel 37:27, Paul is reflecting his conviction that the original covenant promises and the prophetic expectation of their realization after the judgment

---

7. Beale, *The Temple and the Church's Mission*, 353-56; Tim Chester, *From Creation to New Creation: Making Sense of the Whole Bible Story* (The Good Book Company, 2012), 65-68.
8. Peter Walker writes, "Paul's conflation of Old Testament texts in the second passage quoted... is remarkable. Texts which originally applied to physical Israel (Lev. 26:12; Jer. 32:38; Ezek. 37:27) are now applied to those born *outside* the boundaries of ethnic Israel... For Paul something new and irreversible has taken place: the formation of a new 'people of God' in and through Israel's Messiah." *Jesus and the Holy City*, 121.

of the Exile are now beginning to be fulfilled in the Corinthian church!"[9]

Paul then quotes three warnings from Isaiah 52:11, which in its original context is about Israel separating from Babylon as God brings about a new exodus. The gospel of God's reign will be accomplished through the suffering servant (Isa. 53). Paul applies this kingdom passage to Gentiles. And he adds a phrase from Ezekiel 20:34: "then I will welcome you" which draws on a context about God welcoming back Israel when they return from exile.

Paul then conflates two more passages. The Davidic covenant stated that God would be a Father to the son of David. Paul turns the singular "son" to "sons." He can do this because he sees the Davidic covenant in light of the whole canon. Now, we are "sons" because we are "in" the Son. Jesus, as the Jewish Messiah, is a corporate personality.[10] He represents all of His people. Not only that, He adds "and daughters" from Isaiah 43:6, which is about the new exodus God will accomplish for Israel. God would gather the exiles together to Himself: "I will say to the north, Give up, and to the south, Do not withhold; bring my sons from afar and my daughters from the end of the earth" (Isa. 43:6). Israel's deliverance from exile is happening through the Davidic

---

9. Hafemann, *Second Corinthians*, 284.
10. As Moo puts it, "Christians inherit the blessings of God's kingdom only through, and in, Christ. We, 'the sons of God,' are such by virtue of our belonging to *the* Son of God; and we are heirs of God only by virtue of our union with the one who is *the* heir of all God's promises." *Romans*, 505; idem., *Galatians*, 268.

descendent who has descendants, namely the Christian Church.[11]

Then, in an unfortunate chapter break, he tells the Corinthians, "Since we have these promises..." (2 Cor. 7:1). All these promises are for the Corinthians. Wait a minute, I thought he started the letter by saying that all the promises of God are yes in Christ (2 Cor. 1:20). Yes and amen! What is true of the Messiah is true of His people.[12] Jesus fulfills the promises, and He shares them with all who are "in Him." If you are of Christ, then you are a son of Abraham and heirs of his promises (Gal. 3:29). These promises are ultimately for the Church; they are "ours." *We* have these promises. The Church is the end-time Israel by virtue of her union with Israel's Messiah.

## THE NEW HUMANITY

Ephesians 2:11-3:6 is one of the clearest passages of Scripture on the Church/Israel question. It reads,

> Therefore remember that at one time you Gentiles in the flesh, called "the uncircumcision" by what is called the circumcision, which is made in the flesh by hands—

---

11. James Scott writes, "Thus, the Davidic promise is interpreted as a promise of restoration associated with the second exodus," *Second Corinthians* (Grand Rapids: Baker, 1998), 157.
12. This is why Richard Hays refers to a Christocentric and an Ecclesiocentric hermeneutic. *Echoes of Scripture*, 84-121. Similarly, LaRondelle writes, "In biblical typology it is not Christ alone who is the antitype but *Christ and His people*, united in an unbreakable, organic unity, in God's saving purpose for the world." *The Israel of God in Prophecy*, 52. Storms, *Kingdom Come*, 16.

remember that you were at that time separated from Christ, alienated from the commonwealth of Israel and strangers to the covenants of promise, having no hope and without God in the world. But now in Christ Jesus you who once were far off have been brought near by the blood of Christ. For he himself is our peace, who has made us both one and has broken down in his flesh the dividing wall of hostility by abolishing the law of commandments expressed in ordinances, that he might create in himself one new man in place of the two, so making peace, and might reconcile us both to God in one body through the cross, thereby killing the hostility. And he came and preached peace to you who were far off and peace to those who were near. For through him we both have access in one Spirit to the Father. So then you are no longer strangers and aliens, but you are fellow citizens with the saints and members of the household of God, built on the foundation of the apostles and prophets, Christ Jesus himself being the cornerstone, in whom the whole structure, being joined together, grows into a holy temple in the Lord. In him you also are being built together into a dwelling place for God by the Spirit. For this reason I, Paul, a prisoner for Christ Jesus on behalf of you Gentiles— assuming that you have heard of the stewardship of God's grace that was given to me for you, how the mystery was made known to me by revelation, as I have written briefly. When you read this, you can perceive my insight into the mystery of

Christ, which was not made known to the sons of men in other generations as it has now been revealed to his holy apostles and prophets by the Spirit. This mystery is that the Gentiles are fellow heirs, members of the same body, and partakers of the promise in Christ Jesus through the gospel."

Let's just hit the high points. Gentiles *were* at one time alienated from the citizenship (*politeias*) of Israel and strangers to the covenant of promise. But now in Christ, Gentiles who *were* once far off have been brought near. Jesus has made both Jews and Gentiles one. He abolished the Law "to create in himself one new humanity out of the two" (Eph. 2:15 NIV). The Church and Israel are no longer distinct. In the new age, there is now one new humanity. The two are one because of the work of Christ. Jews and Gentiles have now been reconciled "in one body." Gentiles are no longer "strangers and aliens" but are now "fellow citizens" (*sympolitai*) with Israel. Gentiles were once alienated from citizenship in Israel but are now co-citizens. This is all very clear stuff. Gentiles are now included within the Israel of God. As Howard Marshall puts it, "Israel is enlarged to include believing Gentiles."[13] Then Paul speaks of the mystery made known to him, "that the Gentiles are fellow heirs, members of the same body, and partakers of the promise in Christ Jesus through the gospel" (Eph. 3:6). This

---

13. I. Howard Marshall, *New Testament Theology: Many Witnesses, One Gospel* (Downers Grove: IVP Academic, 2004), 384.

is the same mystery of Romans 11 above. It was less clear before, but now it has been made known. Before Christ, Gentiles were strangers to the promise, but are now co-heirs and partakers of the promise. Before Christ, Gentiles were alienated from citizenship in Israel, but now they are part of the same body. Paul's teaching here "...could not be more clear in its portrayal of a unitary people of God in the Messiah, Jesus."[14] In the new age of Christ and the Spirit, there is *total* equality between Jews and Gentiles.

Later, in a move similar to the one he made in 1 Corinthians 5:1 and 12:2, Paul writes that the Ephesians "must no longer walk as the Gentiles (*ethnē*) do" (Eph. 4:17). After Christ, the Ephesians are no longer Gentiles. Paul says something similar in 1 Corinthians 10, when he says, "Give no offense to Jews or to Greek or to the church of God" (1 Cor. 10:32).

## UNBLEMISHED LIGHTS OF THE WORLD

Paul speaks to the Philippian church as the renewed Israel. Remember that Israel was called to be a light to the nations, the vehicle through which God would save the world, but she failed miserably. Philippians 2:14-15 says,

> Do all things without grumbling or disputing, that you may be blameless and innocent, children of God without blemish in the midst of a crooked and twisted

---

14. Wright, "A Christian Approach to Old Testament Prophecy Concerning Israel," 8.

generation, among whom you shine as lights in the world.

In calling the Philippians to no grumbling (*goggysmōn*), he is clearly alluding to the wilderness generation of Israel who, when faced with opposition and hardship, complained and doubted God's goodness. The Lord said, "How long shall this wicked congregation grumble (*goggyzousin*) against me" (Num. 14:27)? In Jewish thought, grumbling came to represent a life in opposition to God (Sir. 10:25, 46:7, Ps of Sol. 5:15, 16:11). The renewed Israel, the community of the new covenant, is to be different from unfaithful Israel of old. They are to be innocent, children of God, without blemish in the midst of a crooked and twisted generation.

Provocatively, Paul describes the pagan world (crooked and twisted) with OT language about old covenant Israel. Deuteronomy 32:5-6 says, "His people have acted corruptly toward Him; this is their defect – they are not His children but a devious and crooked generation. Is this how you repay the LORD, you foolish and senseless people? Isn't He your Father and Creator? Didn't He make you and sustain you?" In Deuteronomy we see that Israel was blemished (*mōmēta*), crooked, and perverse (*skolias kai destrammenēs*), but in Philippians we see that the renewed Israel is to be unblemished (*amōma*) in the midst of a crooked and perverse generation (*skolias kai diestrammenēs*).[15] Israel according the

---

15. Frank Thielman, *Paul and the Law* (Downers Grove, IL: IVP, 1994), 157; Pate, et al., *The Story of Israel*, 228.

flesh was worldly, but the renewed Israel, what he will call "the circumcision" in the next chapter, is to be distinct from the world.

Then Paul applies the vocation of Israel to the Church. They are to be "lights in the world" (Phil. 2:15, Isa. 49:6). Unlike Israel, who was more like the nations than a light to the nations, the Church is to be a beacon and signpost of what the kingdom looks like. The true vocation of God's people, to be a means of blessing the world, is now coming to fruition because of the work of Christ and His Spirit.

## THE CHURCH IS THE CIRCUMCISION

As in Romans 2, Paul redefines what it means to be Jewish around Christ and the Spirit in Philippians 3:

> Look out for the dogs, look out for the evildoers, look out for those who mutilate the flesh. For we are the circumcision, who worship by the Spirit of God and glory in Christ Jesus and put no confidence in the flesh. (Phil. 3:2–3)

Paul warns his readers of those who were teaching that the Gentile Philippians needed to add obedience to the Law to be a true child of God. He calls the false teachers dogs! Dogs in Paul's day weren't domestic pets but unclean scavengers. These false teachers were emphasizing good works, but Paul says their works are evil. They were pushing circumcision, and Paul calls them mutilators of the flesh. He is basically calling them pagans who would butcher their own flesh in order to try and manipulate their gods (Lev. 19:28, 21:5, 1 Kin. 18:28).[16]

Then, in a startling reversal, Paul says "we are the circumcision." Who is the "we?" He goes on to define the "we" as the Church: those who worship by the Spirit of God. We must always remember that the Spirit is a new covenant gift (Ezek. 36:25-27, 37:6, 14). Those who worship by the Spirit are the new covenant people. Those who glory in Christ Jesus. Those who have left all to follow their King. Those who put no confidence in the flesh. Those who know there is no need to add to what Jesus has done. In other words, Christians. The Church is the circumcision, which is another way of saying that the Church is Israel.

Paul actually says that we are "*the* circumcision." It is no accident that Paul never uses "true Israel" or "new Israel." The Church does not replace Israel. The Church is the fulfillment of Israel.[17] Through the work of Christ and the Spirit, Israel has been transformed and expanded to include Gentiles.

## NEITHER JEW NOR GREEK (AGAIN)

Colossians 3:11 says, "Here there is not Greek and Jew, circumcised and uncircumcised, barbarian, Scythian, slave, free; but Christ is all, and in all." Again, this should be shouted

---

16. Wright, *Justification*, 142.
17. Commenting on 1 Corinthians, Richard B. Hays writes, "It is no accident that Paul never uses expressions such as 'new Israel' or 'spiritual Israel.' There always has been and always will be only one Israel. Into that one Israel Gentile Christians such as the Corinthians have now been absorbed." *Echoes of Scripture*, 96-97.

from the rooftops in this discussion: in the new age there is not Greek and Jew! There is not circumcised and uncircumcised! To say, "Yes there is," is to be at cross-purposes with the message of the NT. Since all people are included in "circumcised or uncircumcised," Paul could have stopped there, but he goes further to emphasize just how inclusive the people of God are in the new age. Barbarians were those who lived in the far South. Scythians were the people of the far North and were viewed as the most barbaric savages of the known world. So when Paul says "barbarian, Scythian," he is referring to the nations of the far north and the far south. Then he says there is no slave or free. Paul covers all the bases: the national, religious, geographical, and the social.[18] These distinctions no longer matter among "God's chosen" (Col. 3:12 echoing Isa. 43:20). Christ is all and in all (Col. 3:11).

## NEW COVENANT COMMUNITY

In 1 Thessalonians 4, almost in passing, Paul has yet another passage soaked in Hebrew history.[19] Paul is calling the Thessalonians to purity and cannot help but allude to his favorite new covenant passages to remind them of their identity as he gives moral instruction. He writes,

> Therefore whoever disregards this, disregards not man but God, who gives his Holy Spirit to you. Now

---

18. Bauckham, *Bible and Mission*, 68-69.
19. T.J. Deidun, *New Covenant Morality in Paul* (Rome: Biblical Institute Press, 1981), 19-24, 33, 53, 86, 228.

concerning brotherly love you have no need for anyone to write to you, for you yourselves have been taught by God to love one another. (1 Thess. 4:8–9)

The phrase "who gives his Holy Spirit to you" (*didonta to pneuma autou to hagion eis hymas*) is quoted directly from Ezekiel 37:6 (*dōsō pneuma mou eis hymas*) and Ezekiel 37:14 (*dōsō to pneuma mou eis hymas*). Ezekiel 37 comes right after the new covenant promise that God would replace stony hearts with hearts of flesh that will respond to the Lord rightly. Chapter 37 is the vision of Israel as a valley of dry bones. But God breathes His Spirit and raises them from the dead, gathers Israel into one, and puts the Davidic King over them. It is a passage about the end of Israel's exile. Israel will be raised from the dead. Paul is alluding to this new covenant restoration promise. The Thessalonians are empowered by God as the new covenant people who have already been given new life and are now able to live lives pleasing to the Lord.

The phrase "taught by God" (*theodidaktoi*) is made up by the Apostle, but we should not be surprised to find that he is reflecting on new covenant/new exodus/Kingdom promises. Isaiah 54 is about the eternal covenant of peace that God will ratify when He comes to rescue His people, establish His rule, and dwell with redeemed Israel. Isaiah 54:13 says, "All your children shall be taught by the Lord (*didaktous theou*), and great shall be the peace of your children." And recall that Jeremiah's famous new covenant promise said that in that day, "no longer shall each one teach his neighbor and each his brother, saying 'Know the LORD,' for they shall all know me" (Jer. 31:34). Paul is alluding to these promises which now belong to the Thessalonians. They are the community of the Kingdom which the prophets promised. They have been taught by God, and therefore they are to be a community characterized by mutual love.

## THE RAPTURE

While not directly addressing the Church/Israel question, Dispensational interpreters use 1 Thessalonians 4:17 for their program. In their system, God's "plan A" is Israel, and for Him to get back to that, He must get the Church out of the way. The rapture pulls the Church out of the picture, closing the parentheses so God can get on with ethnic Israel. This is the *only* passage that refers to the rapture and they misread it.[20] There is nothing here about a secret rapture of the Church. Three reasons make this clear.

First, there is nothing secret about this coming. The context shows that there will be a shout, an archangel's voice, and a trumpet. Unless we are dealing with a sort of "Christian dog whistle" here, Paul's point is that this is going to be a very loud event; certainly not a secret one.

Second, if the secret pre-tribulation rapture view is right,

---

20. The word "rapture" comes from the Latin *rapiemur*, which comes from the Greek *harpagēsometha*. Sometimes Dispensationalists appeal to Matt. 24:36-44, but there, those "taken" are taken in judgment, just as in Noah's day. See Benjamin L. Merkle, "Who Will Be Left Behind? Rethinking the Meaning of Matthew 24:40-41 and Luke 17:34-35," *Westminster Theological Journal* 72 (2010).

Paul's encouragement (and the main purpose of this passage) would be strange. The confused Thessalonian Christians were concerned that the Day of the Lord had already happened (1 Thess. 5:1-2). They were worried about their brothers and sisters who had already died. But if the Dispensational view is right, all Paul would have had to say was, "Look around, sillies, we are still here on earth so of course the secret rapture has not occurred yet."

Third, and most importantly, the word for "meet" (*apantēsin*) was a popular one in the Greek world. It was a word used when a visiting dignitary came to town (Matt. 25:6, Acts 28:15-16). Much like today, if the President came to town, we wouldn't just let him mosey on in. The people of the city would go out of the city "to meet" him and escort him into town to his desired destination. Paul plunders imperial vocabulary here to say that when the Lord loudly returns, we who are alive will be raptured—meeting Him in the air—in order to escort the King to His renewed earth, where we will be with Him forever.

# 11

# The Letters

We now turn to a few key passages in the rest of the NT letters that bear on the Church/Israel question.

## THE NEW COVENANT COMMUNITY

Hebrews could be summed up as "Jesus is better." More specifically, the new covenant He inaugurates is better than the old covenant. He begins by showing that Jesus is the climactic revelation of God. In these last days, He has spoken to us by His Son. Then He shows how the revelation of the Son is superior to old covenant revelation. Jesus is superior to angels. (Jews believed that angels were associated with the giving of the Law. Cf. Heb. 2:2, Gal. 3:19, Acts 7:53, Deut. 33:2 LXX.) He is better than Moses (Heb. 3). He brings the rest the wilderness generation never attained (Heb. 4). He is the eternal priest according to the order of Melchizedek (Heb. 7). He brings about a better covenant.

Hebrews 8 includes the longest quotation of the OT in the NT. He quotes Jeremiah's promise of the new covenant:

> But as it is, Christ has obtained a ministry that is as much more excellent than the old as the covenant he mediates is better, since it is enacted on better promises. For if that first covenant had been faultless, there would have been no occasion to look for a second. For he finds fault with them when he says: "Behold, the days are coming, declares the Lord, when I will establish a new covenant with the house of Israel and with the house of Judah, not like the covenant that I made with their fathers on the day when I took them by the hand to bring them out of the land of Egypt. For they did not continue in my covenant, and so I showed no concern for them, declares the Lord. For this is the covenant that I will make with the house of Israel after those days, declares the Lord: I will put my laws into their minds, and write them on their hearts, and I will be their God, and they shall be my people. And they shall not teach, each one his neighbor and each one his brother, saying, 'Know the Lord,' for they shall all know me, from the least of them to the greatest. For I will be merciful toward their iniquities, and I will remember their sins no more." In speaking of a new covenant, he makes the first one obsolete. And what is becoming obsolete and growing old is ready to vanish away." (Heb. 8:6–13)

Jeremiah knew that Israel needed something more. Israel was stiff-necked, and only a fresh work of God to fully and finally forgive their sins would enable them to obey. The author of Hebrews shows that Jesus brings about that covenant and it applies to the Church. This is what we celebrate in communion (Luke 22:20). We are the people of the new covenant.[1] The new covenant promises are fulfilled in the Church.[2]

## KINGDOM OF PRIESTS

Recall that in the old covenant God said that if Israel obeyed they would be "a kingdom of priests and a holy nation" (Exod. 19:6). This was to be their missional vocation. Priests mediate between God and the world, and the whole nation was to be a kingdom of priests. They were to be holy and

---

1. Ryrie's pointing to the lack of a definite article before "new covenant" is special pleading. His solution of two new covenants is as well. *Dispensationalism*, 204. Progressive Dispensationalists argue that there is an "already/not yet" dimension to the new covenant, so that the church benefits from the spiritual aspects *already*, but the *not yet* aspects pertaining to ethnic Israel await the millennium. Ironically, some Covenant Theologians argue for an "already/not yet" dimension of the new covenant as well. For them, the spiritual aspects are the *already*, but the promise that all in the covenant community is part of the *not yet*. On the Dispensational side, see Michael Vlach, *Has the Church Replaced Israel?* (Nashville: B&H Academic, 2010), 158. On the covenant theology side, see Richard Pratt, "Infant Baptism in the New Covenant," in *The Case for Covenantal Infant Baptism* ed. Gregg Strawbridge (Phillipsburg, NJ: P&R, 2003), 156-74. NCT concludes that these are theological presuppositions driving inaugurated eschatology.
2. Storms writes, "The true Israel of this eschatological age is no longer the nation of the old covenant, but the Christian community, inaugurated by a new covenant through a mediator greater than the Israelite priesthood; for Jesus not only repeats the work of prophet, priest and king, but in him it is perfected. In this new community the hopes of the Old Testament Israel are fulfilled." *Kingdom Come*, 41.

a light to the nations. Without full forgiveness and the new covenant gift of the Spirit, they could not fulfill this calling.

But the Church, the community of the new covenant, can and does. Peter writes,

> But you are a chosen race, a royal priesthood, a holy nation, a people for his own possession, that you may proclaim the excellencies of him who called you out of darkness into his marvelous light. Once you were not a people, but now you are God's people; once you had not received mercy, but now you have received mercy." (1 Pet. 2:9–10)

Peter applies Israel's labels to the Church.[3] The Church is now the chosen race (Isa. 43:20), the kingdom of priests (Exod. 19:6), the holy nation (Deut. 7:6), and the people for His own possession (Isa. 43:21, Mal. 3:17).[4] This is also part of

---

3. This is a good place to remind the reader that this book is far from exhaustive. We are only hitting high points. Much more could be said about the application of Israel's labels to the Church: saints, flock, chosen, beloved, children, house, etc. Though I could not acquire this book, see Charles D. Provan, *The Church is Israel Now: Old and New Testament Scripture Texts Which Illustrate the Conditional Privileged Position and Titles of 'Racial Israel' and their Transfer to the Christian Church* (Vallecito, CA: Ross House Books, 1987).

4. Wayne Grudem writes, "God has bestowed on the church almost all the blessings promised to Israel in the Old Testament. The dwelling place of God is no longer the Jerusalem Temple, for Christians are the new 'temple' of God... The priesthood able to offer acceptable sacrifices to God is no longer descended from Aaron, for Christians are now the true 'royal priesthood' with access before God's throne (vv. 4-5, 9). God's chosen people are no longer said to be the people of God, for Christians - both Jewish Christians and Gentile Christians - are now 'God's people' (v. 10a) and those who have 'received mercy' (v. 10b). Moreover, Peter takes these quotations from contexts which repeatedly warn that God will reject his people who persist in rebellion against him, who reject the precious 'cornerstone' which he has established. What more could be needed in order to say with assurance that the

the fulfillment of what we saw in Isaiah 66, where foreigners would be priests of the Lord when the kingdom comes (Isa. 66:21).

Peter, like Paul, in Romans 9, quotes Hosea in the phrase, "once you were not a people, but now you are God's people." We saw that in Hosea God would judge Israel but would then restore them. Peter and Paul believe that the restoration of Israel is happening through the international Church.[5]

And don't miss the purpose of the people of God: *that you may proclaim His excellencies.* Blessed to be a blessing.[6] The people of God experience privilege and obligation. The international Church of Jesus Christ is both the result of and the means by which God is restoring Israel.

---

church has now become the true Israel of God." *1 Peter* (Grand Rapids: Eerdmans, 1988), 113.

5. Thomas R. Schreiner writes, "Peter saw these promises as fulfilled in Jesus Christ, and God's elect nation is no longer coterminous with Israel but embraces the Church of Jesus Christ, which is composed of both Jews and Gentiles… Again the privileges belonging to Israel now belong to the church of Jesus Christ. The church does not replace Israel, but it does fulfill the promises made to Israel; and all those, Jews and Gentiles, who belong to the true Israel are now part of the new people of God." *1, 2 Peter, Jude* (Nashville: B&H, 2003), 114, 115; LaRondelle similarly writes, "Peter declares that Hosea's prophecy of God's future restoration of Israel has now been fulfilled in Christ's universal church!" *The Israel of God in Prophecy*, 106.

6. N.T. Wright writes, "Peter takes the basic Israel vocation and declares boldly that it has not become the fulfilled-Israel vocation. 'Fulfilled Israel' means, primarily, Jesus himself, Israel's Messiah, but the vocation then extends to all those who follow and belong to him. Jesus is the one true 'living stone,' and his followers are the 'living stones' by which the true Temple is to be built, bringing the presence of God into the wider world, carrying forward the mission of declaring God's powerful and rescuing acts, and beginning the work of implementing the messianic rule of Jesus in all the world. That is what it means to be a 'royal priesthood'." *After You Believe* (New York: HarperOne, 2010), 86.

## SYNAGOGUE OF SATAN

Like Peter, John also applies the labels and vocation of Israel to the Church (Rev. 1:5, 5:10). John has harsh words for those Jews who were persecuting the Church. He writes, "I know your tribulation and your poverty (but you are rich) and the slander of those who say that they are Jews and are not, but are a synagogue of Satan" (Rev. 2:9). He says much the same in Revelation 3:9. Jesus said the same to the unbelieving Jews: "You are of your father the devil, and your will is to do your father's desires" (John 8:44). In line with the rest of the theology of the NT, being a Jew is no longer about ethnicity. John says that these ethnically Jewish people are not Jews because they are opposed to the Jewish Messiah and His people.[7] In fact, to be opposed to Jesus and His people makes one a "synagogue" of Satan.

## NEW JERUSALEM

At the end of his book, John speaks of the old and new Jerusalem. Old Jerusalem is described as the great prostitute and the New Jerusalem is described as the bride.[8] In Revelation 17:1-3, one of the seven angels carries John away in the Spirit, and then he sees the woman sitting on the beast (Rome). And he saw the woman, "drunk with the blood of

---

7. Hays writes, "The interesting point here is that the author of Revelation contends that such people are not really Jews at all; the obvious implication, here as in Philippians 3:2-3, is that the 'real Jews' are those who confess Jesus as Lord." *The Moral Vision of the New Testament*, 411.
8. The imagery of Jerusalem as a prostitute is, of course, nothing new. Cf. Jer. 2:20-25, 32-37, 3:1-14, Ezekiel 16.

the saints, the blood of the martyrs of Jesus" (Rev. 17:6). Jesus had warned Jerusalem, saying:

> Therefore I send you prophets and wise men and scribes, some of whom you will kill and crucify, and some you will flog in your synagogues and persecute from town to town, so that on you may come all the righteous blood shed on earth, from the blood of righteous Abel to the blood of Zechariah the son of Barachiah, whom you murdered between the sanctuary and the altar. Truly, I say to you, all these things will come upon this generation. (Matt. 23:34–36; cf. Acts 7:52, Luke 11:50-51)

Then in Revelation 21:9-10, using similar language, one of the seven angels carries John away in the Spirit to show him "the Bride, the wife of the Lamb." And the angel showed him the holy city Jerusalem coming down out of heaven from God. What is often missed is that the New Jerusalem is a people, not a place.[9] The old unfaithful Jerusalem has fallen and the New Jerusalem has been inaugurated. As Leithart puts it, "John's visions in Revelation, then, build on Jesus' prophecies about the destruction of the temple and city of Jerusalem, and they show that Jesus is going to build a new city and marry a new Bride."[10]

---

9. See Robert H. Gundry, "The New Jerusalem: People as Place, Not Place for People," *Novum Testamentum* 29.3 (1987): 254-264; Dalrymple, *These Brothers of Mine*, 60, 73.
10. Peter J. Leithart, *A House for My Name: A Survey of the Old Testament* (Moscow, ID: Canon Press, 2000), 249.

# 12

# Synthesis and Conclusion

Let's tie all this up. God creates all things good, but His image-bearers think they know better than Him, distrust His good Word, and utter ruin follows. He calls an old barren couple to sort it all out. Through the offspring of Abraham, God will undo what Adam did, defeating evil and blessing the nations. Abraham's family is taken out of Egypt, but God must do a new work to take Egypt out of Abraham's family. They were supposed to be the solution to the problem, but they merely add to it. They were called to bless the nations by being a light, but their lives are full of darkness. Rather than seeing themselves as elect to bless, they see themselves as elite to spurn. Israel wants a king like the nations, but God gives them a man after His own heart and promises His son an eternal kingdom. Their idolatry only increases. So God sends the prophets to warn of impending judgment. But judgment won't be the last word. God will use judgment to purify His people. The Lord announces through His prophets that He will return, inspect His temple, judge His enemies, rescue His people, gather the exiles, forgive their sin, transform them from the inside out, and dwell among them as their King. Then Israel will be and do what she was meant to be and do. God would send Elijah to warn them before He comes. Elijah comes in John the Baptist. God follows in the Prophet from Nazareth. He reconstitutes Israel around Himself and sends them out to proclaim good news and be witnesses. God is restoring Israel through the expansion of the international Church. The kingdom has come and the King sends heralds out to announce it. This is the chief task of the community of the new covenant.

It should be obvious that this worldview is at odds with Dispensationalism. In many ways Dispensationalism has a different storyline than New Covenant Theology. Their view that God has two peoples simply will not stand under the scrutiny of sacred Scripture. We have looked at passage after passage that affirms there is one people of God, and that Israel has been reshaped, expanded, and extended to include any and all who receive Israel's Messiah as Lord and Savior. The warp and woof of the vision of the NT is that Jews and Gentiles are one in Christ Jesus. To insist on the opposite is to do great damage to the storyline of Scripture.

I think the heart of the problem is that they miss the purpose of God in calling Israel. As we saw in Genesis 12, God was never merely interested in Israel for Israel's sake. God's purpose was always to *bless the nations* through Israel.

"Israel was called to be the means by which God redeemed the nations."[1]

As mentioned earlier, the view advocated in this book is much closer to traditional Covenant Theology, but it is not identical. One difference is how we view union with Christ and how it affects those who are in Christ.[2] In the old covenant, all one had to do to enter the covenant community was to be born and circumcised. The sign of circumcision is to be applied to Abraham and his offspring, and their offspring, and their offspring. So every member of the old covenant community had their male infants circumcised. Covenant Theologians will then argue that, based on the over-arching "covenant of grace," this *genealogical principle* ("and to your offspring") remains the same across the old and new covenants.[3] The believer applies the sign of the covenant, now baptism, to their infants.[4]

We differ here. Because of Christ, everything is transformed, including the genealogical principle.[5] He brings about a new covenant. Jeremiah has said that in the new covenant *all* will know the Lord.[6] Jesus—not the individual

---

1. Dalyrymple, *These Brothers of Mine*, 133.
2. See my *Union With Christ: Last Adam and Seed of Abraham* (Frederick, MD: New Covenant Media, 2012); Moore, *Kingdom of Christ*, 149; Gentry and Wellum, *Kingdom Through Covenant*, 121-22.
3. R. Fowler White, "The Last Adam and His Seed: An Exercise in Theological Preemption," *Trinity Journal* 6.1 (Spring 1985), 60; Wellum and Gentry, *Kingdom Through Covenant*, 63, 70, 121, 125,608, 695.
4. See Wellum, "Relationship Between the Covenants."
5. White says, "the genealogical principle continues without revocation but not without reinterpretation under the new covenant." "The Last Adam and His Seed," 70; Wellum, "Relationship Between the Covenants," 137.
6. In other words, the new covenant will entail a regenerate Church membership. It

believer—is the mediator of the new covenant, and the sign is to be applied to *His* offspring, not the offspring of individual Christians.[7] The children of Jesus are spiritual, not physical. Jesus has no grandchildren. Christ brings about more significant changes in the covenant community than Covenant Theology allows.

So believers are united to Christ by faith and *then* become children of Abraham. It is not that Israel = Church, but Israel = Christ = Those in Christ (Church).[8] Union with Christ is the key. And only those who have trusted in Christ are part of the Church.[9]

Notice the irony here. To make a slight overstatement, both Covenant Theology and Dispensationalism view the Abrahamic covenant as if Christ had never come. Oddly, they share the same hermeneutic, Dispensationalism with land and Covenant Theology with offspring.[10] Both fail to see how

---

will no longer be a "mixed community." Note the honesty of Charles Hodge: "In order to justify the baptism of infants, we must attain and authenticate such an idea of the Church as that it shall include the children of believing parents." *Systematic Theology* (Grand Rapids: Eerdmans, 1970), 546-47.

7. White, "The Last Adam and His Seed," 66 n. 13.
8. Poythress, a covenant theologian, agrees: "The argument is strongest if one does not bluntly and simplistically assert that the church is a straight-line continuation of Israel. Rather one proceeds by way of Christ himself as the center point of fulfillment of the promises." *Understanding Dispensationalists*, 126. But by affirming this, he undermines his own position regarding infant baptism because one is united to Christ by faith.
9. Baptists who bind themselves to The Second London Baptist Confession of Faith (1689) may agree with me on this point. I am referring to Westminsterian Covenant Theology.
10. Reisinger is worth quoting at length on this point: "Both the Dispensationalist and the Covenant Theologian want to bring the promise of Abraham and his seed into the present age in a *physical* sense via the lineage of their physical children. They both insist that the promise made to Abraham and his seed is an unconditional covenant and is therefore still in effect for physical seeds. The Dispensationalist naturalizes

significant Jesus and the fulfillment He brings is.[11] Dispensationalism views the land promise and the nation of Israel without Christ-centered lenses; Covenant Theology views the genealogical principle without Christ-centered lenses on.[12] The aim of New Covenant Theology is to view all of Scripture and all of history with Christocentric lenses firmly in place. We must not minimize who Jesus is and what He has done.[13] Rather, we must be stubbornly concentrated on Him.

---

the seed to mean physical Israel, and the Paedobaptist naturalizes the seed to mean the physical children of believers. The Paedobaptist wants to make the Abrahamic covenant to be a special covenant with believers concerning the salvation of their *physical* children that is still in effect today. The Dispensationalist want the same covenant to be a special covenant still in force with Jews concerning the land of Palestine. In the end, the Paedobaptist does exactly the same thing with Abraham's seed as the Dispensationalist! He merely does it for a different purpose." *Abraham's Four Seeds*, 94. Also see 5, 36, 47, 53, 58, 99, 100, 118; Wellum and Gentry, *Kingdom Through Covenant*, 63, 69 n. 91, 76, 86, 113, 117-18, 122, 704 n. 115, 706 n. 121.

11. Regarding the Dispensational tendency to look past the reality for the shadows, Wright says, "The attempt to say that there are some parts of the Old Testament (relating to Jerusalem, Land or Temple) which have not yet been 'fulfilled' and so need a historical and literal 'fulfillment' now, or at some other time, is an explicit attempt to take something away from the achievement of Christ in his death and resurrection, and to reserve it for the work of human beings in a different time and place. The work of Christ is once again 'incomplete'." "Jerusalem," 74. Sam Storms calls this "redemptive regression." *Kingdom Come*, 21, 25.
12. With Covenant Theology, one could add the Sabbath to the genealogical principle, but that would take us too far off topic.
13. Merkle, "Old Testament Prophecies Regarding the Nation of Israel," 21, 22.

## 13

# So What?

Okay, so the renewed Israel includes Gentiles. So what? Does all this biblical theology make a difference when the rubber meets the road? Absolutely. Let's conclude by looking at seven ways these truths affect our everyday lives.

### TRUTH

First is the matter of truth. If there were no nitty-gritty practical implications, correctly understanding God's Word still matters. If the rubber never met the road, understanding God through His Word still matters. In our age of anti-intellectualism, theology is often frowned upon, but our King calls us to love the Lord our God with all of our minds. We need to rightly understand God and His plans and purposes. Though my list of "life verses" is always growing, Colossians 1:9-14 is at the top of the list. There, Paul prays that the Colossians would be "filled with the knowledge of his will in all spiritual wisdom and understanding" (Col. 1:9). The knowledge of His will is not where we should work, go to college, who to marry, etc. It refers to His plans and purposes in this world to make Christ preeminent. We need to *understand* this with all *wisdom* and *understanding*. But the point of the understanding is to walk worthy of the Lord "bearing fruit in every good work and increasing in the knowledge of God" (Col. 1:10). Understand, so as to walk, so as to increase in understanding. Truth matters.

## IDENTITY

Rightly understanding the Church as the fulfillment of Israel affects our vision of who we are. We are the people of God. The history of Israel is our history (1 Cor. 10:1). We are those on whom the end of the ages has come (1 Cor. 10:11).[1] The Church is the end-time people of God. I think too many Christians have a way too small view of the Church.[2] It is through the Church that "the manifold wisdom of God might

---

1. Hays writes, "The church discovers its true identity only in relation to the sacred story of Israel, and the sacred story of Israel discovers its full significance – so Paul passionately believed – only in relation to God's unfolding design for salvation of the Gentiles in the church." *Echoes of Scripture in the Letters of Paul*, 100-01; James W. Aageson, *Written Also for Our Sake: Paul and the Art of Biblical Interpretation* (Louisville: Westminster/John Knox Press, 1993), 84.
2. Commenting on 2 Corinthians 6:14-7:1, Hafemann writes, "The realization that God's final stage in redemptive history has begun should fuel our work to purify the church. The last days of God's unfolding plan for the world are here. In the midst of this evil age, God is establishing outposts of the kingdom in anticipation of the return of Christ. God has a plan for the world – and the church is it! Believers need a bigger picture of who they are. J.B. Phillip's famous line, 'Your God is too small' needs a sequel, 'Your Church is too small,' not in terms of numbers, but in terms of her self-understanding. The people of the new covenant have cosmic significance as the people of the last days of God's unfolding plan for the world." *Second Corinthians*, 293.

now be made known to the rulers and authorities in the heavenly places" (Eph. 3:10).

Our identity informs our actions. We must know who we are and whose we are in the biblical drama to play our part faithfully. We saw this in 2 Corinthians 6 and 1 Thessalonians 4. In the former, we are to remain pure because we are the end-time people of God among whom the Lord of glory dwells (2 Cor. 6:14-7:1). Because the OT promises of Israel's restoration are ours, we need to live like it and urgently follow the Lord. In the latter, we see that because we are the new covenant community, we should remain pure and continue to sacrificially love one another (1 Thess. 4:8-9). We are the restored Israel.

## HOPE

Seeing the Church as the renewed and restored Israel should transform our understanding of Christian hope. Jesus is the sole heir because He was the sole obedient Israelite. All of God's promises are yes in Him (2 Cor. 1:20). So all the OT promises funnel down to the singular Seed of Abraham (Gal. 3:16), who in turn re-opens the funnel to include any and all who trust in Him. Now, Gentiles in the Messiah are heirs of Israel's promises. We are co-heirs with the King (Rom. 8:17).

We saw above that our inheritance is much more than "pie in the sky when we die." We also saw that to focus our hope on a rapture or a slim piece of land in the middle east is far too small a hope. Our inheritance is ultimately the whole renovated world. We will reign with Christ our King on the new earth. Let's leave behind *Left Behind* and embrace a more robust and biblical hope.

## RACISM

We have seen repeatedly that in the economy of God, it is grace—not race—that matters. This understanding should serve as kryptonite to racism (and patriotism for that matter). The people of God are international. All nations are included in the people of God. None are superior to others.[3] In the new covenant, there are two and only two "classes" of people: those "in Adam" and those "in Christ." Circumcision counts for nothing, and neither does uncircumcision (Gal. 5:6, 6:15, 1 Cor. 7:19).

## OBEDIENCE

Because God has kept His promise to pour the Spirit upon Israel in the last days, the new covenant community is able to obey from the heart. As John Reisinger likes to say, "The old covenant did not come with batteries included." The new covenant brings heart transformation. The divine heart surgeon is in business. So now we are able and expected to please the Lord with the way we live. This means we will be a "contrast society."[4] Because we follow Jesus, our lives look different. We show the world what life under the rule of King Jesus looks like.

The heart of the call of the new covenant is the call to love.

---

3. See J. Daniel Hays, *From Every People and Nation: A Biblical Theology of Race* (Downers Grove: InterVarsity Press, 2003).
4. Goheen, *Light to the Nations*, 8, 208-11.

But it's not a squishy kind of love, it's a cross-shaped love.[5] It's bloody. "This is how we know what love is: Jesus Christ laid down his life for us. And we ought to lay down our lives for our brothers and sisters" (1 John 3:16 NIV). In fulfillment of Isaiah's and Jeremiah's prophecies about Israel, the Church has been "taught by God" *in order to* love one another (1 Thess. 4:9, Isa. 54:10, Jer. 31:33-34). This self-giving love, more than anything else, is how the world will know we are disciples of Jesus (John 13:34-35).

## PRAISE

Understanding God's plan for Israel and the inclusion of the nations into Israel should lead to praise. Laying out the mystery of God including Gentiles in the root of Israel leads Paul to blurt out:

> Oh, the depth of the riches and wisdom and knowledge of God! How unsearchable are his judgments and how inscrutable his ways! For who has known the mind of the Lord, or who has been his counselor? Or who has given a gift to him that he might be repaid? For from him and through him and to him are all things. To him be glory forever. Amen. (Rom. 11:33–36)

This should also lead us Gentiles to praise God for His grace. We should be as astounded by and grateful for God

---

5. See my *Theological Foundations for New Covenant Ethics* (Frederick, MD: New Covenant Media, 2013), 69-134; *The Imitation of Jesus* (Frederick, MD: New Covenant Media, 2014).

including Gentiles in His plan as we are about justification by grace through faith alone. We do not deserve a seat at this table. We "were at that time separated from Christ, alienated from the commonwealth of Israel and strangers to the covenants of promise, having no hope and without God in the world. But now in Christ Jesus you who once were far off have been brought near by the blood of Christ. For he himself is our peace, who has made us both one" (Eph. 2:12-14). Because of the work of Jesus, we are now fellow citizens in Israel. Here is John's vision of the appropriate response to the Lord for his salvation of the nations:

> After this I looked, and behold, a great multitude that no one could number, from every nation, from all tribes and peoples and languages, standing before the throne and before the Lamb, clothed in white robes, with palm branches in their hands, and crying out with a loud voice, "Salvation belongs to our God who sits on the throne, and to the Lamb!" And all the angels were standing around the throne and around the elders and the four living creatures, and they fell on their faces before the throne and worshiped God, saying, "Amen! Blessing and glory and wisdom and thanksgiving and honor and power and might be to our God forever and ever! Amen." (Rev. 7:9–12)

## MISSION

Finally, mission. I treat this one last because I think the

implications of this study are largest for the Church's mission. The purpose of Israel was missional. They were called to be the means by which God would save the world. They were to be a light to the nations, but were instead like the nations and hid the light under a basket (Luke 8:16). They buried their one talent (Matt. 25:14-30) rather than being faithful stewards. They were "entrusted with the oracles of God" (Rom. 3:2), but rather than drawing the nations in, the name of God was blasphemed among the Gentiles because of them (Rom. 2:24).

This is one of the reasons why Jesus has such sharp words for Israel and her leaders. They had forgotten the point of their existence! In launching the kingdom, Jesus "seeks to gather and purify Israel for the sake of the nations, to restore Israel to take up its missional calling."[6] "Jesus' own mission is to restore an eschatological community that takes up that missional role and identity again."[7] We are the restored Israel commissioned with the task of gathering in the exiles (Mark 13:27) and summoning the nations to submit to the Lordship of King Jesus (Matt. 28:18-20). We are fishers of men. We have been redeemed and now are the agents of the end-time restoration of Israel.[8]

---

6. Michael F. Bird, "'A Light to the Nations' (Isaiah 42:6 and 49:6): Inter-textuality and Mission Theology in the Early Church," *The Reformed Theological Review* 65.3 (December 2006), 126.
7. Goheen, *A Light to the Nations*, 76.
8. France, *The Gospel According to Mark*, 536; "The gathering of the nations into the kingdom of God is a characteristic activity of the *eschaton*, the last days. As Jesus's ministry begins, so does the eschaton, and those whom Jesus gathers to him join him in gathering yet others into the salvation of the kingdom of God." Goheen, *A light to the Nations*, 83.

New covenant Israel does not exist for itself. We are *sent* for the nations. We are "the restored Israel-for-the-world."[9] "God's new people in Christ are also a people for the sake of the world."[10] Because of the work of Christ and the Spirit, we will be faithful in this vocation. In fulfillment of the vision of Isaiah 49, we are now the light of the world called to let it shine (Matt. 5:14). We live in this "time between the times" for the sake of mission. This is the "era of witness."[11] Lesslie Newbigin is so bold as to say that if the Church fails to see the missionary nature of our existence between the two comings of Christ, we have a false eschatology![12]

More could be said, but I hope you see that this is an important conversation with many implications. In conclusion, I hope your mind has been stimulated, and that even if not convinced, King Jesus has become more central to your thinking and life. He has done and is doing a great work!

~ *SOLI DEO GLORIA* ~

---

9. N.T. Wright, *The Last Word* (New York: HarperOne, 2005), 49; Pate, et al., *The Story of Israel*, 281.
10. Wright, *The Mission of God*, 391.
11. "Thus in the time between the testaments, Israel awaits the coming kingdom, during which time God will gather Israel back and finally it will fulfill its missional calling. *And God does act:* he brings the kingdom to Israel in the person of Jesus. With the coming of Jesus, the promised gathering of God's eschatological people begins." *A Light to the Nations*, 75-76.
12. Lesslie Newbigin quoted in Goheen, *A Light to the Nations*, 126.

# Works Cited

Aageson, James W. *Written Also for Our Sake: Paul and the Art of Biblical Interpretation.* Louisville: Westminster/John Knox Press, 1993.

Alexander, T.D. "Genealogies, Seed and the Compositional Unity of Genesis." *Tyndale Bulletin* 44.2: 255-367. November, 1993.

_____. "Royal Expectations in Genesis to Kings: Their Importance for Biblical Theology." *Tyndale Bulletin* 49.2: 191-212. November 1998.

Bauckham, Richard. *Bible and Mission.* Grand Rapids: Baker Academic, 2003.

Beale, G.K. *A New Testament Biblical Theology: The Unfolding of the Old Testament in the New.* Grand Rapids: Baker Academic, 2011.

_____. *The Temple and the Church's Mission: A Biblical Theology of the Dwelling Place of God. NSBT.* Downers Grove, IL: InterVarsity Press, 2004.

Bird, Michael F. "'A Light to the Nations' (Isaiah 42:6 and 49:6): Inter-textuality and Mission Theology in the Early Church. *The Reformed Theological Review* 65.3: 122-31. December 2006.

Blaising, Craig and Darrell Bock. *Dispensationalism, Israel and the Church.* Grand Rapids: Zondervan, 1992.

_____. *Progressive Dispensationalism*. Grand Rapids: Baker Books, 1993.

Bruno, Christopher R. "The Deliverer From Zion: The Source(s) and Function of Paul's Citation in Romans 11:26-27. *Tyndale Bulletin* 59.1: 119-34. 2008.

Burge, Gary M. *Jesus and the Land: The New Testament Challenge to "Holy Land" Theology*. Grand Rapids: Baker Academic, 2010.

Caird, G.B. *Jesus and the Jewish Nation*. London: The Athlone Press, 1965.

Chester, Tim. *From Creation to New Creation: Making Sense of the Whole Bible Story*. The Good Book Company. 2012.

Ciampa, Roy. E. "The History of Redemption." In *Central Themes in Biblical Theology*. Edited by Scott J. Hafemann and Paul R. House. Grand Rapids: Baker Academic, 2007.

Cowan, Christopher W. "Context is Everything: 'The Israel of God' in Galatians 6:16." *The Southern Baptist Journal of Theology* 14.3: 78-85. Fall 2010.

Dalrymple, Rob. *These Brothers of Mine: A Biblical Theology of Land and Family and a Response to Christian Zioinism*. Eugene, OR: Wipf and Stock, 2015.

Deidun, T.J. *New Covenant Morality in Paul*. Rome: Biblical Institute Press, 1981.

Dempster, Stephen G. *Dominion and Dynasty: A Theology of the Hebrew Bible*. NSBT. Downers Grove, IL: InterVarsity Press, 2003.

Dickson, John. *The Best Kept Secret of Christian Mission*. Grand Rapids: Zondervan, 2010.

Diffey, Daniel S. "The Royal Promise in Genesis." *Tyndale Bulletin* 62.2: 313-16. 2011.

# WORKS CITED

Dumbrell, William J. *Covenant and Creation: A Theology of the Old Testament Covenants*. Carlisle, PA: Paternoster Press, 1984.

———. *The Faith of Israel: A Theological Survey of the Old Testament*. Grand Rapids: Baker Academic, 2002.

———. *The Search for Order: Biblical Eschatology in Focus*. Eugene, OR: Wipf and Stock Publishers, 1994.

Fee, Gordon D. *The First Epistle to the Corinthians*. NICNT. Grand Rapids: Eerdmans, 1987.

France, R.T. *Divine Government: God's Kingship in the Gospel of Mark*. Vancouver: Regent College Publishing, 1990.

———. *Jesus the Radical: A Portrait of the Man They Crucified*. Vancouver: Regent College Publishing, 1989.

———. "Old Testament Prophecy and the Future of Israel: A Study of the Teaching of Jesus." *Tyndale Bulletin* 26: 53-78. 1975.

———. *The Gospel of Mark*. NIGTC. Grand Rapids: Eerdmans, 2002.

———. *The Gospel of Matthew*. NICNT. Grand Rapids: Eerdmans, 2007.

Gentry, Peter G. and Stephen J. Wellum. *Kingdom Through Covenant: A Biblical-Theological Understanding of the Covenants*. Wheaton: Crossway, 2012.

Goheen, Michael W. *A Light to the Nations: The Missional Church and the Biblical Story*. Grand Rapids: Baker Academic, 2011.

Goldsworthy, Graeme. *Preaching the Whole Bible as Christian Scripture*. Grand Rapids: Eerdmans, 2000.

Grudem, Wayne. *First Peter*. TNTC. Grand Rapids: Eerdmans, 1988.

Gundry, Robert H. "New Jerusalem: People as Place, Not Place for People." *Novum Testamentum* 29.3: 254-64. 1987.

Hafemann, Scott J. *Second Corinthians*. NIVAC. Grand Rapids: Zondervan, 2000.

Hatina, Thomas R. "The Focus of Mark 13:24-27: The Parousia, or the Destruction of the Temple?" *Bulletin for Biblical Research* 6: 43-66. 1996.

Hays, J. Daniel. *From Every People and Nation: A Biblical Theology of Race*. NSBT. Downers Grove: InterVarsity Press, 2003.

Hays, Richard B. *Echoes of Scripture in the Letters of Paul*. London: Yale University Press, 1989.

_____. *First Corinthians*. Louisville: John Knox Press, 1997.

_____. "The Canonical Matrix of the Gospels." In Stephen C. Barton, *The Cambridge Companion to the Gospels*. Cambridge: Cambridge University Press, 2006.

_____. *The Moral Vision of the New Testament*. New York: HarperOne, 1996.

_____. *Reading Backwards: Figural Christology and the Fourfold Gospel Witness*. Waco: Baylor University Press, 2014.

Hodge, Charles. *Systematic Theology*. Grand Rapids: Eerdmans, 1970.

Horne, Charles M. "The Meaning of the Phrase 'And Thus All Israel Will Be Saved'." *JETS* 21.4: 329-334. December 1978.

Kaiser, Jr., Walter C. "The Blessing of David: The Charter for Humanity." In John H. Skilton, *The Law and the Prophets: Old Testament Studies in Honor of Oswald Thompson Allis*. Philipsburg, NJ: Presbyterian and Reformed Publishing, 1974.

Kirk, J.R. Daniel. "Conceptualising Fulfilment in Matthew." *Tyndale Bulletin* 59.1: 77-98. 2008.

Kostenber, Andreas J. and Peter T. O'Brien. *Salvation to the Ends of the Earth: A Biblical Theology of Mission*. NSBT. Downers Grove: InterVarsity Press, 2001.

LaRondelle, Hans K. *The Israel of God in Prophecy: Principles of Prophetic Interpretation*. Berrien Springs, MI: Andrews University Press, 1983.

# WORKS CITED

Lee, Chee-Chiew "[Nations] and the Abrahamic Promise of Blessings for the Nations." *JETS* 52.3: 467-82. September 2009.

Leithart, Peter J. *A House for My Name: A Survey of the Old Testament.* Moscow, ID: Canon Press, 2000.

———. *The Four: A Survey of the Gospels.* Moscow, ID: Canon Press, 2010.

Lohfink, Gerhard. *Does God Need the Church? Toward a Theology of the People of God.* Translated by Linda M. Maloney. Collegeville, MN: Liturgical Press, 1999.

Longenecker, Bruce W. *The Triumph of Abraham's God: The Transformation of Identity in Galatians.* Nashville: Abingdon Press, 1998.

Marcus, Joel. *The Way of the Lord: Christological Exegesis of the Old Testament in the Gospel of Mark.* Louisville: Westminster/John Knox Press, 1992.

Marshall, I. Howard. "Acts." In *Commentary on the New Testament Use of the Old Testament.* Edited by G.K. Beale and D.A. Carson. Grand Rapids: Baker Academic, 2007.

———. *New Testament Theology: Many Witnesses, One Gospel.* Downers Grove, IL: IVP Academic, 2004.

Mathison, Keith A. *Dispensationalism: Rightly Dividing the People of God?* Phillipsburg, NJ: P&R Publishing, 1995.

Merkle, Ben L. "Old Testament Restoration Prophecies Regarding the Nation of Israel: Literal or Symbolic?". *The Southern Baptist Journal of Theology* 14.1: 14-25. Spring 2010.

———. "Romans 11 and the Future of Ethnic Israel." *JETS* 43.4: 709-21. December 2009.

———. "Who Will Be Left Behind? Rethinking the Meaning of Matthew 24:40-41 and Luke 17:34-35." *Westminster Theological Journal* 72: 169-79. 2010.

Meyer, Jason C. *The End of the Law: Mosaic Covenant in Pauline Theology*. Nashville: B&H Academic, 2009.

Moo, Douglas J. *Galatians. BECNT.* Grand Rapids: Baker Academic, 2013.

———. *The Epistle to the Romans. NICNT.* Grand Rapids: Eerdmans, 1996.

Moore, Russell. "Personal and Cosmic Eschatology." In *A Theology for the Church.* Edited by Daniel L. Akin. Nashville: B&H Academic, 2007.

———. *The Kingdom of Christ.* Wheaton: Crossway, 2004.

Motyer, S. "Israel (nation)." In *New Dictionary of Biblical Theology.* Edited by T. Desmond Alexander and Brian S. Rosner: 581-87. Downers Grove: InterVarsity Press, 2000.

Mouw, Richard J. *When the Kings Come Marching In: Isaiah and the New Jerusalem.* Grand Rapids: Eerdmans, 2002.

Pao, David W. *Acts and the Isaianic New Exodus.* Grand Rapids: Baker Academic, 2000.

Pate, C. Marvin, J. Scott Duvall, J. Daniel Hays, E. Randolph Richards, W. Dennis Tucker, Jr., and Preben Vang. *The Story of Israel: A Biblical Theology.* Downers Grove: IVP Academic, 2004.

Peterson, David G. *Transformed by God: New Covenant Life and Ministry.* Downers Grove: IVP Academic, 2012.

Poythress, Vern S. *Understanding Dispensationalists.* Phillipsburg, NJ: P&R Publishing, 1994.

Pratt Jr., Richard L. "Infant Baptism in the New Covenant." In *The Case for Covenantal Infant Baptism.* Edited by Gregg Strawbridge. Phillipsburg, NJ: P&R Publishing, 2003.

Provan, Charles D. *The Church is Israel Now: Old and New Testament Scripture Texts Which Illustrate the Conditional Privileged Position and Titles of 'Racial Israel' and their Transfer to the Christian Church.* Vallecito, CA: Ross House Books, 1987.

Reisinger, John G. *Abraham's Four Seeds: A Biblical Examination fo the Presuppositions of Covenant Theology and Dispensationalism.* Frederick, MD: New Covenant Media, 1998.

————. *But I Say Unto You.* Frederick, MD: New Covenant Media, 2006.

Riddlebarger, Kim. *Amillennialism: Understanding the End Times.* Grand Rapids: Baker, 2003.

Robertson, O. Palmer. "Is There a Distinctive Future for Ethnic Israel in Romans 11". In *Perspectives on Evangelical Theology.* Edited by Kenneth S. Kantzer and Stanley N. Gundry. Grand Rapids: Baker, 1979.

————. *The Israel of God: Yesterday, Today, and Tomorrow.* Phillipsburg, NJ: P&R Publishing, 2000.

————. *Understanding the Land of the Bible: A Biblical-Theological Guide.* Phillipsburg, NJ: P&R Publishing, 1996.

Ryrie, Charles C. *Dispensationalism.* Chicago: Moody, 2007.

Schreiner, Thomas R. *1, 2 Peter, Jude.* NAC. Nashville: B&H, 2003.

————. *Galatians.* ZECNT. Grand Rapids: Zondervan, 2010.

————. *New Testament Theology: Magnifying God in Christ.* Grand Rapids: Baker Academic, 2008.

————. *Romans.* BECNT. Grand Rapids: Baker Academic, 1998.

Scott, James M. *Second Corinthians.* Grand Rapids: Baker, 1998.

Storms, Sam. *Kingdom Come: The Amillennial Alternative.* Scotland: Mentor, 2013.

Stott, John, *Understanding the Bible.* Grand Rapids: Zondervan, 1984.

Tiede, David L. Tiede. "The Exaltation of Jesus and the Restoration of Israel in Acts 1." *Harvard Theological Review* 79.1-3: 278-86. January/April/July, 1986.

# WORKS CITED

Thielman, Frank. *Paul and the Law*. Downers Grove: InterVarsity Press, 1994.

Thompson, Alan. *The Acts of the Risen Lord Jesus. NSBT*. Downers Grove: InterVarsity Press, 2011.

Treat, Jeremy R. *The Crucified King: Atonement and Kingdom in Biblical and Systematic Theology*. Grand Rapids: Zondervan, 2014.

Vlach, Michael J. *Has the Church Replaced Israel?: A Theological Evaluation*. Nashville: B&H Academic, 2010.

Walker, P.W.L. *Jesus and the Holy City: New Testament Perspectives on Jerusalem*. Grand Rapids: Eerdmans, 1996.

Watts, Rikki E. *Isaiah's New Exodus in Mark*. Grand Rapids: Baker Academic, 1997.

_____. "Mark." In *Commentary on the New Testament Use of the Old Testament*. Edited by G.K. Beale and D.A. Carson. Grand Rapids: Baker Academic, 2007.

Wellum, Stephen J. "Baptism and the Relationship Between the Covenants." In *Believer's Baptism: Sign of the New Covenant in Christ*. Edited by Thomas R. Schreiner and Shawn D. Wright: 97-161. Nashville: B&H Academic, 2006.

White, A. Blake. *Galatians: A Theological Interpretation*. Frederick, MD: New Covenant Media, 2011.

_____. *Missional Ecclesiology*. Frederick, MD: New Covenant Media, 2013.

_____. *The Abrahamic Promises in Galatians*. Frederick, MD: New Covenant Media, 2013.

_____. *The Imitation of Jesus*. Frederick, MD: New Covenant Media, 2014.

_____. *Theological Foundations for New Covenant Ethics*. Frederick, MD: New Covenant Media, 2013.

## WORKS CITED

———. *Union With Christ: Last Adam and Seed of Abraham.* Frederick, MD: New Covenant Media, 2012.

———. *What is New Covenant Theology: An Introduction.* Frederick, MD: New Covenant Media, 2012.

White, R. Fowler. "The Last Adam and His Seed: An Exercise in Theological Preemption." *Trinity Journal 6.1.* Spring 1985.

Williamson, Paul. "Abraham, Israel, and the Church." *The Evangelical Quarterly,* 72.2: 99-118. April-June 2000.

———. "Covenant." In *New Dictionary of Biblical Theology.* Edited by T. Desmond Alexander and Brian S. Rosner: 419-29. Downers Grove: InterVarsity Press, 2000.

———. *Sealed With An Oath: Covenant in God's Unfolding Purpose.* NSBT. Downers Grove: InterVarsity Press, 2007.

Wright, Christopher J.H. "A Christian Approach to Old Testament Prophecy Concerning Israel." In *Jerusalem Past and Present in the Purposes of God.* Edited by P.W.L. Walker: 1-19. Cambridge: Tyndale House, 1992.

———. *The Mission of God.* Downers Grove, IL: IVP Academic, 2006.

Wright, N.T. *After You Believe: Why Christian Character Matters.* New York: HarperOne, 2010.

———. *How God Became King: The Forgotten Story of the Gospels.* New York: HarperOne, 2011.

———. "Jerusalem in the New Testament." In *Jerusalem Past and Present in the Purposes of God.* Edited by P.W.L. Walker: 53-77. Cambridge: Tyndale House, 1992.

———. *Jesus and the Victory of God.* Minneapolis: Fortress Press, 1996.

———. *Justification: God's Plan and Paul's Vision.* Downers Grove: IVP Academic, 2009.

## WORKS CITED

_____. *Paul and the Faithfulness of God.* Minneapolis: Fortress Press, 2013.

_____. *The Climax of the Covenant: Christ and the Law in Pauline Theology.* Minneapolis: Fortress Press, 1993.

_____. *The Last Word: Scripture and the Authority of God.* New York: HarperOne, 2005.

_____. *The New Testament and the People of God.* Minneapolis: Fortress Press, 1992.

_____. *The Resurrection of the Son of God.* Minneapolis: Fortress Press, 2003.

_____. *What Saint Paul Really Said.* Grand Rapids: Eerdmans, 1997.

# Other Books by A. Blake White

*The Newness of the New Covenant*
*The Law of Christ: A Theological Proposal*
*Galatians: A Theological Interpretation*
*Abide in Him: A Theological Interpretation of John's First Letter*
*Union with Christ: Last Adam and Seed of Abraham*
*What is New Covenant Theology? An Introduction*
*Theological Foundations for New Covenant Ethics*
*The Abrahamic Promises in Galatians*
*Missional Ecclesiology*
*The Imitation of Jesus*
*Joyful Unity in the Gospel: The Call of Philippians*

# About Cross to Crown Ministries

At *Cross to Crown Ministries*, our motivation is simple. We want to encourage believers to live purposefully with explicit devotion to Jesus Christ in every facet of life. This includes Bible study, teaching, marriage, parenting, worship, working, playing, learning, retirement planning, or anything else we do.

There are several distinct facets to our ministry. The *New Covenant School of Theology* trains pastors, elders, lay leaders, and any interested Christian from the Christ-centered perspectives of New Covenant Theology and Biblical Theology. We also produce resources——written, audio, and video—to help you think and live intentionally Christianly. We hold conferences to bring Christians together for intensive Christ-centered preaching and teaching. We produce music to be used for personal and public worship and edification in the hope that our intentionally Christ-exalting, New Covenant-oriented songs will spur Christians to love and good deeds for His glory and praise. Our website

## ABOUT CROSS TO CROWN MINISTRIES

(www.crosstocrown.org) is the one-stop location for all of our ministries and resources.

Made in the USA
Middletown, DE
15 April 2017

> "I can't wait to get this book into the hands of my seminary students."
>
> Douglas Goodin, President of New Covenant School of Theology

# THE TRUTH MAY SURPRISE YOU

What do you think, are the Jews still God's chosen people? Is your answer based more on theological tradition or the clear teaching of Scripture? In other words, how would you make your case from the Bible?

In *God's Chosen People*, theologian and pastor A. Blake White makes his biblical case that "Jesus Christ and His people are the fulfillment of all OT prophecy," even the prophecies about the Jews. Now that Christ has come, it's about your faith, not your family tree. Actually, that was God's plan all along.

Blake White (M.Div. SBTS, Th.M SWBTS) is a campus pastor for Austin Ridge Bible Church in Austin, Texas. He has written more than ten books on various theological and exegetical issues. He and his lovely wife Alicia have 4 children: Josiah, Asher, Karis, and Knox.

CROSS TO CROWN MINISTRIES
5210 Centennial Blvd, Colorado Springs, CO 80919
www.crosstocrown.org

ISBN 9780985118785

*Suzanne Maiden provides hard-hitting evidence that we never die and our loved ones always reach back to comfort us.
A must read!*
—**Mark Anthony** the Psychic Lawyer®

# Spirit
## *Untethered*

### A Psychotherapist's Journey from Terminal Cancer to Seeing the Dead

SUZANNE GRACE MAIDEN